Course

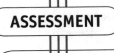

Assessment Alternatives

Holistic Scoring: Prompts and Models

Rubrics for
- writing assignments
- optional projects
- oral and visual literacy projects and performances

Portfolio Management

Inventory Forms

Evaluation Forms

HOLT, RINEHART AND WINSTON

A Harcourt Classroom Education Company

Austin · New York · Orlando · Atlanta · San Francisco · Boston · Dallas · Toronto · London

STAFF CREDITS

EDITORIAL

Director
Mescal Evler

Manager of Editorial Operations
Bill Wahlgren

Executive Editor
Emily Shenk

Project Editor
Megan Truex

Prototyping Editor
Cheryl Christian

Contributing Editors
Jane Archer Feinstein, Ann Michelle Gibson, Sean W. Henry, Errol Smith, Tressa Sanders

Copyediting
Michael Neibergall, *Copyediting Manager;* Mary Malone, *Senior Copyeditor;* Joel Bourgeois, Elizabeth Dickson, Gabrielle Field, Jane Kominek, Millicent Ondras, Theresa Reding,

Kathleen Scheiner, Laurie Schlesinger, *Copyeditors*

Project Administration
Marie Price, *Managing Editor;* Lori De La Garza, *Editorial Operations Coordinator;* Thomas Browne, Heather Cheyne, Diane Hardin, Mark Holland, Marcus Johnson, Jill O'Neal, Joyce Rector, Janet Riley, Kelly Tankersley, *Project Administration;* Gail Coupland, Ruth Hooker, Margaret Sanchez, *Word Processing*

Editorial Permissions
Janet Harrington, *Permissions Editor*

Writers of Exemplary Student Essays
Adrian González, Paul Feinstein, David Thompson, Jr.

ART, DESIGN AND PHOTO

Graphic Services

Kristen Darby, *Manager*

Image Acquisitions
Joe London, *Director;* Tim Taylor, *Photo Research Supervisor;* Rick Benavides, *Assistant Photo Researcher;* Elaine Tate, *Supervisor;* Erin Cone, *Art Buyer*

Cover Design
Sunday Patterson

PRODUCTION

Belinda Barbosa Lopez, *Senior Production Coordinator*
Simira Davis, *Supervisor*
Nancy Hargis, *Media Production Supervisor*
Joan Lindsay, *Production Coordinator*
Beth Prevelige, *Prepress Manager*

MANUFACTURING

Michael Roche, *Supervisor of Inventory and Manufacturing*

Dr. Roger Farr, author of the essay that appears on pages 1–23, is currently Chancellor's Professor of Education and Director of the Center for Innovation and Assessment at Indiana University. He is a past president of the International Reading Association and the author of both norm-referenced tests and performance assessments. Dr. Farr has taught at both elementary and high school levels in New York State and has served as a school district reading consultant.

The International Reading Association presented Dr. Farr the William S. Gray award for outstanding lifetime contributions to the teaching of reading in 1984. He was elected to the IRA for outstanding lifetime contributions to the teaching of reading in 1984. He was elected to the IRA Reading Hall of Fame in 1986 and was selected by the IRA as the Outstanding Teacher Educator in Reading in 1988.

Printed in the United States of America

ISBN 0-03-057577-X

12345 179 04 03 02 01 00

Table of Contents

Table of Contents

Forms for tracking student improvement in reading

Peer and self-assessment forms for recording student writing, establishing baselines, and setting goals

Table of Contents

Forms for tracking student improvement in writing

Peer and self-assessment forms for recording student speaking and listening activities, establishing baselines, and setting goals

Forms for tracking student improvement in speaking and listening

Table of Contents

Table of Contents

About This Book

This booklet, *Assessment Alternatives*, accompanies the *Elements of Language* series and provides assessment resources for portfolio work, essays written in testing situations, and a variety of classroom activities.

Part I | ## Portfolio Management

This section begins with an essay designed to provide an introduction to portfolio work, including suggestions about how to develop and use portfolios and how to conduct conferences with students about their work.

The introductory essay is followed by a set of student forms for assessing and organizing portfolio contents and for setting goals for future work. Also included is a set of teacher forms for communicating with parents or guardians about student work and for generally assessing students' progress.

Part II | ## Inventories and Evaluation Forms

These forms can be used to record work, to establish baselines and goals, and to think critically about student work in a variety of areas. These areas include:

- **Reading**
- **Writing**
- **Speaking and Listening**
- **Viewing and Representing**
- **Cooperative Learning**

The goal of these forms is to encourage students to develop criteria for assessing their work and to identify areas for improvement. Many forms can also be used for assessment of a peer's work.

A set of forms for the teacher to use in assessing student progress can be found after the set of student forms for each content area.

Part III | ## Writing Assessment

This section contains three different kinds of rubrics for assessing on-demand writing: *Six Point Scales*, *Four Point Scales*, and *Six Trait Scales*. Accompanying these scales are high-level, mid-level, and low-level examples of student writing. Individual evaluations, based on each of the three rubrics, follow each student essay.

Part IV | ## Evaluation Rubrics

Included in this section are sets of criteria for evaluating all *Focus On* workshops and *Choices* activities included in the pupil's edition. These rubrics may be used by students for peer or self-assessment or by the teacher for assessing student work.

Portfolio Assessment in the Language Arts

Although establishing and using a portfolio assessment system requires a certain amount of time, effort, and understanding, an increasing number of teachers believe that the benefits of implementing such a system richly reward their efforts.

Language arts portfolios are collections of materials that display aspects of students' use of language. They are a means by which students can collect samples of their written work over time so that they and their teachers can ascertain how the students are developing as language users. Because reflection and self-assessment are built-in aspects of language arts portfolios, both also help students develop their critical-thinking and metacognitive abilities.

Each portfolio collection is typically kept in a folder, box, or other container to which items are added on a regular basis. The collection can include a great variety of materials, depending on the design of the portfolio assessment program, the kinds of projects completed inside and outside of the classroom, and the interests of individual students. For example, portfolios may contain student stories, essays, sketches, poems, letters, journals, and other original writing, and they may also contain reactions to articles, stories, and other texts the student has read. Other materials that are suitable for inclusion in portfolios are drawings, photographs, audiotapes, and videotapes of students taking part in special activities; clippings and pictures from newspapers and magazines; and notes on favorite authors and on stories and books that the student hopes to read. Many portfolios also include several versions of the same piece of writing, demonstrating how the writing has developed through revision.

Finally, portfolios may contain logs of things the student has read or written, written reflections or assessments of portfolio work, and tables and explanations about the way the portfolio is organized. (A collection of forms that can be used to generate these items may be found on page 24 following this essay and in Part II of this booklet.)

The Advantages of Portfolio Assessment

How can portfolio assessment help you meet your instructional goals? Here are some of the most important advantages of using portfolios:

- *Portfolios link instruction and assessment.* Traditional testing is usually one or more steps removed from the process or performance being assessed. However, because portfolio assessment focuses on performance—on students' actual use of language—portfolios are a highly accurate gauge of what students have learned in the classroom.

- *Portfolios involve students in assessing their own language use and abilities.* Portfolio assessment can provide some of the most effective learning opportunities available in your classroom. In fact, the assessment is

Portfolio Assessment in the Language Arts *(continued)*

itself instructional: Students, as self-assessors, identify their own strengths and weaknesses. Furthermore, portfolios are a natural way to develop metacognition in your students. As the collected work is analyzed, the student begins to think critically about how he or she makes meaning while reading, writing, speaking, and listening. For example, the student begins to ask questions while reading, such as "Is this telling me what I need to know?" "Am I enjoying this author as much as I expected to?" "Why or why not?" While writing, the student may ask, "Am I thinking about the goals I set when I was analyzing my portfolio?" That's what good instruction is all about: getting students to use the skills you help them develop.

- *Portfolios invite attention to important aspects of language.* Because most portfolios include numerous writing samples, they naturally direct attention to diction, style, main idea or theme, author's purpose, and other aspects of language that are difficult to assess in other ways. The portfolio encourages awareness and appreciation of these aspects of language as they occur in literature and nonfiction as well as in the student's own work.

- *Portfolios emphasize language use as a process that integrates language behaviors.* Students who keep and analyze portfolios develop an understanding that reading, writing, speaking, listening, viewing, and representing are all aspects of a larger process. They come to see that language behaviors are connected by thinking about and expressing one's own ideas and feelings.

- *Portfolios make students aware of audience and the need for a writing purpose.* Students develop audience awareness by regularly analyzing their portfolio writing samples. Evaluation forms prompt them to reflect on whether they have defined and appropriately addressed their audience. Moreover, because portfolios provide or support opportunities for students to work together, peers can often provide feedback about how well a student has addressed an audience in his or her work. Finally, students may be asked to consider particular audiences (parents, classmates, or community groups, for example) who will review their portfolios; they may prepare explanations of the contents for such audiences, and they may select specific papers to present as a special collection to such audiences.

- *Portfolios provide a vehicle for student interaction and cooperative learning.* Many projects that normally involve cooperative learning produce material for portfolios. Portfolios, in turn, provide or support many opportunities for students to work together. Students

As they become attuned to audience, students automatically begin to be more focused on whether their work has fulfilled their purpose for writing. They begin to ask: "Did I say what I meant to say? Could I have been clearer and more effective? Do I understand what this writer wants to tell me? Do I agree with it?" Speaking and listening activities can also be evaluated in terms of audience awareness and clarity of purpose.

Portfolio Assessment in the Language Arts *(continued)*

can work as partners or as team members who critique each other's collections. For example, students might work together to prepare, show, and explain portfolios to particular audiences, such as parents, administrators, and other groups interested in educational progress and accountability.

- ***Portfolios can incorporate many types of student expression on a variety of topics.*** Students should be encouraged to include materials from different subject areas and from outside school, especially materials related to hobbies and other special interests. In this way, students come to see language arts skills as crucial tools for authentic, real-world work.

- ***Portfolios provide genuine opportunities to learn about students and their progress as language users.*** Portfolio contents can reveal to the teacher a great deal about the student's background and interests with respect to reading, writing, speaking, listening, viewing, and representing. Portfolios can also demonstrate the student's development as a language user and reveal areas where he or she needs improvement.

How to Develop and Use Portfolios

As you begin designing a portfolio program for your students, you may wish to read articles and reports that discuss the advantages of portfolio assessment. The reading list on page 23 can help you get started.

Basic Design Features

For a portfolio program to be successful in the classroom, the program should reflect the teacher's particular instructional goals and the students' needs as learners. Teachers are encouraged to customize a portfolio program for their classrooms, although most successful portfolio programs share a core of essential portfolio management techniques. Following are suggestions that teachers will want to consider in customizing a portfolio program.

- *Integrate portfolio assessment into the regular classroom routine.* Teachers should make portfolio work a regular class activity by providing opportunities for students to work with their collections during class time. During these portfolio sessions, the teacher should promote analysis (assessment) that reflects his or her instructional objectives and goals.

- *Link the program to classroom activities.* Student portfolios should contain numerous examples of classroom activities and projects. To ensure that portfolios reflect the scope of students' work, some teachers require that certain papers and assignments be included.

You may want to require that certain papers, projects, and reports be included in the portfolio. Such requirements should be kept to a minimum so that students feel that they can include whatever they consider to be relevant to their language development.

- *Let students have the control.* Students can develop both self-assessment and metacognition skills when they select and arrange portfolio contents themselves. This practice also develops a strong sense of ownership: students feel that their portfolios belong to them, not to the teacher. When students take ownership of their work, they accept more responsibility for their own language development. To encourage a sense of ownership on the part of students, portfolios should be stored where students can get at them easily, and students should have regular and frequent access to their portfolios.

- *Include students' creative efforts.* To ensure that the portfolios develop a range of language skills, encourage students to include samples of their creative writing, pieces they have written outside of class, and publishing activities that they may have participated in, such as the production of a class magazine.

Portfolios that include such planning papers and intermediate drafts are called *working portfolios*. Working portfolios force the student to organize and analyze the material collected, an activity that makes clear to the student that language use is process.

- *Make sure portfolios record students' writing process.* If portfolios are to teach language use as a process that integrates various language behaviors, they need to contain papers that show how writing grows out of planning and develops through revision. Portfolios should include notes, outlines, clippings, reactions to reading or oral presentations, pictures, and other materials that inspired the final product. Equally vital to the

How to Develop and Use Portfolios (continued)

The act of selecting particular papers to show to special audiences—parents, another teacher, or the principal, to name a few—refines students' sense of audience. Preparing and presenting selected collections, called *show portfolios*, engages students in a more sophisticated analysis of their work and encourages them to visualize the audience for the show collection.

If students feel free to include writing and reading done outside of class in their portfolios, you can discover interests, opinions, and concerns that can be touched on during conferences. In turn, by communicating interest in and respect for what engages the student, you can promote the success of the portfolio program.

portfolio collections are the different drafts of papers that demonstrate revision over a period of time. Such collections can promote fruitful, concrete discussions between student and teacher about how the student's process shaped the final product.

- *Rely on reactions to reading and listening.* If portfolios are to link and interrelate language behaviors, students must be encouraged to include reactions to things they read and hear. During conferences, teachers may want to point out how some of the student's work has grown out of listening or reading.

- *Encourage students to consider the audience.* Portfolio building prompts students to think about the audience because, as a kind of publication, the portfolio invites a variety of readers. Students will become interested in and sensitive to the reactions of their classmates and their teacher, as well as to the impact of the collections on any other audiences that may be allowed to view them.

- *Promote collaborative products.* Portfolios can promote student collaboration if the program sets aside class time for students to react to one another's work and to work in groups. This interaction can occur informally or in more structured student partnerships or team responses. In addition, many writing projects can be done by teams and small groups, and any common product can be reproduced for all participants' portfolios. Performance projects, speeches, and other oral presentations often require cooperative participation. Audiotapes and videotapes of collaborative projects may be included in portfolios.

- *Let the portfolios reflect a variety of subject areas and interests.* The language arts portfolio should include material from subject areas other than language arts. Broadening the portfolio beyond the language arts classroom is important if the student is to understand that reading, writing, speaking, and listening are authentic activities—that is, that they are central to all real-world activities. Any extensive attempt to limit portfolio contents may suggest to students that reading and writing skills relate only to the language arts classroom.

Initial Design Considerations

Using what you have read so far, you can make some initial notes as guidelines for drafting your portfolio assessment design. You can complete a chart like the one on the next page to plan how you will use portfolios and what you can do to make them effective.

How to Develop and Use Portfolios *(continued)*

What are my primary goals in developing my students' ability to use language?	How can portfolios contribute to meeting these goals?	What design features can ensure this?

How to Develop and Use Portfolios *(continued)*

Some key considerations for designing a portfolio program have been suggested above. Other considerations will arise as you assess ways to use the portfolios. Here are some questions that will probably arise in the planning stages of portfolio assessment.

How can I introduce students to the concepts of portfolio management?

What examples of student work should go into the portfolios?

What should the criteria be for deciding what will be included?

How and where will the portfolio collections be kept?

Designing a Portfolio Program

How can I introduce students to the concepts of portfolio management?

One way is to experiment with a group of your students. If you use this limited approach, be sure to select students with varied reading and writing abilities to get a sense of how portfolios work for students with a range of skill levels. To introduce portfolio assessment to them, you can either talk to students individually or as a group about what they will be doing. If other students begin expressing an interest in keeping portfolios, let them take part as well. The kind of excitement that builds around portfolio keeping almost guarantees that some students not included initially will want to get on board for the trial run; some may start keeping portfolios on their own.

You might let students help you design or at least plan some details of the system. After explaining both the reasons for keeping portfolios and the elements of the program that you have decided are essential, you can let students discuss how they think certain aspects should be handled. Even if you decide you want students to make important decisions concerning the program's design, you will need to have a clear idea of what your teaching objectives are and of what you will ask students to do.

What examples of student work should go into the portfolios?

Portfolios should reflect as much as possible the spectrum of your students' language use. What you want to ensure is that student self-assessment leads to the understanding that language skills are essential to all learning. For this to happen, portfolios should contain reading, writing, speaking, listening, viewing, and representing activities that relate to a number of subject areas and interests, not just to the language arts. Moreover, the portfolio should include final, completed works as well as drafts, notes, freewriting, and other samples that show the student's thinking and writing process.

FINAL PRODUCTS Students should consider including pieces that are created with a general audience in mind; writing that is communicative and intended for particular audiences; and writing that is very personal and that is used as a method of thinking through situations, evaluating experiences, or musing simply for enjoyment. The portfolios can contain a variety of finished products, including

- original stories, dialogue, and scripts
- poems

How to Develop and Use Portfolios (continued)

- essays, themes, sketches
- song lyrics
- original videos
- video or audio recordings of performances
- narrative accounts of experiences
- correspondence with family members and friends
- stream-of-consciousness pieces
- journals of various types

Examples of various types of journals that students might enjoy keeping are described below.

Keeping Journals

A journal is an excellent addition to a portfolio—and one that teachers report is very successful. Journal keeping develops the habit of recording one's observations, feelings, and ideas. At the same time, journal writing is an excellent way to develop fluency. Specifically, it can help tentative writers to overcome the reluctance to put thoughts down as words. Journal keeping can be a bridge over inhibitions to writing and can become a student's favorite example of his or her language use. All this recommends the addition of journals to the portfolio.

The success with journals in encouraging young writers has led teachers to experiment with a variety of types:

PERSONAL JOURNAL This form of journal allows the writer to make frequent entries (regularly or somewhat irregularly) on any topic and for any purpose. This popular and satisfying kind of journal writing develops writing fluency and reveals to students the essential relationship between thinking and writing. (If the journal is kept in the portfolio, you may wish to remind students that you will be viewing it. Tell students to omit anything they would not be comfortable sharing.)

LITERARY JOURNAL OR READER'S LOG This journal provides a way of promoting open-ended and freewheeling responses to student reading. Students are usually allowed to structure and organize these journals in any way that satisfies them. As a collection of written responses, the literary journal is a valuable source of notes for oral and written expression; it can also give students ideas for further reading. Finally, the literary journal is another tool that reveals to students that reading, writing, and thinking are interrelated.

TOPICAL JOURNAL This style of journal is dedicated to a particular interest or topic. It is a valuable experience for students to be allowed to express themselves freely about a specific topic—a favorite hobby, pastime, or issue, for example.

How to Develop and Use Portfolios *(continued)*

As with the literary journal, the topical journal can point students toward project ideas and further reading.

DIALOGUE JOURNAL For this journal format, students select one person—a classmate, friend, family member, or teacher, for example—to strike up a continuing dialogue with. Dialogue journals help develop audience awareness and can promote cooperative learning. If students in your class are keeping dialogue journals with each other, be prepared to help them decide in whose portfolio the journal will go. (Because making copies may be too time consuming or expensive, you could help students arrange alternate custody, or have them experiment by keeping two distinct journals.)

Fragments and Works in Progress

In addition to finished products, portfolios should include papers showing how your students are processing ideas as readers, writers, speakers, and listeners. Drafts that show how writing ideas are developed through revision are especially helpful as students assess their work. Items that demonstrate how your language users are working with their collections can include

- articles, news briefs, sketches, or other sources collected and used as the basis for written or oral projects. These "seeds" may include pictures created or collected by students and used for inspiration for the subject. The portfolio may also include some items that have not yet been developed.
- reading-response notes that have figured in the planning of a paper and have been incorporated into the final work. Once again, some notes may be intended for future projects.
- other notes, outlines, or evidence of planning for papers written or ready to be drafted
- pieces in which the student is thinking out a problem or considering a topic of interest or behavior or is planning something for the future. These pieces may include pro and con arguments, and persuasive points and reactions to reading.
- freewriting, done either at school or at home
- early versions (drafts) of the latest revision of a piece of writing
- notes analyzing the student's latest draft, which may direct subsequent revision
- solicited reactions from classmates or the teacher
- a published piece accompanied by revised manuscripts showing edits

How to Develop and Use Portfolios (continued)

- correspondence from relatives and friends to which students have written a response or to which students need to respond
- journal or diary entries that are equivalent to preliminary notes or drafts of a piece of writing
- tapes of conversations or interviews to which a piece of writing refers or on which it is based

While test results in general do not make good contents for portfolios, performance assessments can provide a focused example of both language processing and integration of reading and writing skills. Such performance tests are now frequently structured as realistic tasks that require reading, synthesizing, and reacting to particular texts. More often than not, these assessments guide the student through planning stages and a preliminary draft. (These parts of the assessment are rarely rated, but they lend themselves directly to self-analysis and should definitely be included with the final draft.)

What should the criteria be for deciding what will be included?

Teachers often want to ensure that students keep certain kinds of papers in the portfolios, while also affirming students' need for a genuine sense of ownership of their collections. Achieving a balance between these two general objectives may not be as difficult as it seems. Students can be informed at the time that they are introduced to the portfolio concept that they will be asked to keep certain items as one part of the overall project. Almost certainly, it will be necessary to explain at some point that the collections are to be working portfolios and that certain records—including many of the forms provided in this booklet—will also need to be included. As they become accustomed to analyzing the papers in their portfolios, students can be encouraged or required to select the contents of their portfolios, using criteria that they develop themselves. Teachers can help students articulate these criteria in informal and formal conferences. Following are criteria teachers or students might consider:

- papers that students think are well done and that therefore represent their best efforts, or papers that were difficult to complete
- subjects that students enjoyed writing about, or texts they have enjoyed reading; things that they think are interesting or will interest others
- things that relate to reading or writing students intend to do in the future, including ideas that may be developed into persuasive essays, details to support positions on issues, and reaction to favorite literary texts

Discourage the inclusion of workbook sheets, unless they contain ideas for future student writing; they tend to obscure the message that language development is a process, a major component of which is the expression of student ideas and opinions.

You might want to brainstorm a list of things that could be kept in your students' portfolios and then prioritize the items on your list according to which ones you think will be essential for students' development.

How to Develop and Use Portfolios *(continued)*

- papers that contain ideas or procedures that students wish to remember
- incomplete essays or projects that presented some problem for the student. He or she may plan to ask a parent, teacher, or fellow student to react to the work or to earlier drafts.
- work that students would like particular viewers of the portfolio (the teacher, their parents, their classmates, and so on) to see, for some reason. This criterion is one that will dictate selections for a show portfolio; it may also determine some of the papers selected for the overall collection.

After building their collections for some time, students should be able to examine them and make lists of their selection criteria in their own words. Doing so should balance out any requirements the teacher has set for inclusion and should ensure students' sense of ownership.

A final note on selection criteria for student portfolios: While portfolios should certainly contain students' best efforts, too often teachers and students elect to collect only their "best stuff." An overemphasis on possible audiences that might view the collection can make it seem important that the collection be a show portfolio. Preparing show portfolios for particular audiences can require students to assess their work in order to decide what is worth including. That is a worthwhile experience, but once the preparation for the show has been completed, student self-assessment ends.

How and where will the portfolio collections be kept?

Start collecting some samples of holders you can show when you introduce portfolio management to your students. Decorate at least one sample, or have a young friend or relative do it. At the same time, be thinking about areas in your classroom where the collections can be kept.

Part of the fun of keeping portfolios is deciding what the holders for the collections will look like. In a few classrooms, portfolio holders are standardized, but in most classes, the students are allowed to create their own. Many teachers allow students to furnish their own containers or folders, as long as these are big enough to hold the collections without students' having to fold or roll the papers—and not so large as to create storage problems. In addition, many teachers encourage their students to decorate their portfolio holders in unique, colorful, personal, and whimsical ways. Allowing this individuality creates enthusiasm for the project. It also helps students develop a genuine sense of ownership, an important attitude to foster if this system is to succeed.

The kinds of holders that students are likely to bring to school include household cardboard boxes, stationery boxes, folders of various types, paper or plastic shopping bags, computer paper boxes, and plastic and cardboard containers for storing clothing and other items. It would be a good idea to

How to Develop and Use Portfolios *(continued)*

have several different examples to show students when discussing how they will keep their papers. It is also a good idea to have some holders on hand for students who are unable to find anything at home that they think is suitable, and for use as replacements for unworkable holders some students may bring, such as shoe boxes that are too small to hold the portfolio items.

The resulting storage area will probably not be neatly uniform but will not necessarily be unattractive, either. Teachers who want a tidier storage area might find similar boxes to pass out to all students, who are then allowed to personalize them in different ways.

The amount of space available in a particular classroom will, of course, determine where students keep their collections, but it is vital that the area be accessible to students. It will save a great deal of inconvenience during the school year if the portfolios are on open shelves or on an accessible ledge of some kind and are not too far from students. If students can retrieve and put away their portfolios in less than a minute or two, there will be many instances when portfolio work can be allowed. Deciding where to keep the portfolios is a decision that may be put off until students know enough about the process to help make the decision.

Open access to portfolios does create the possibility of students looking at classmates' collections without permission and without warning. It seems only fair to remind students not to include in their portfolio anything they would not want others to see. A caution from the teacher could save a student from a wounding embarrassment.

Conferencing with Students

If you are new at conducting portfolio conferences, ask a student who has kept one or more papers to sit down and talk with you. Talk with the student about what he or she thinks is strong about the paper, how it came to be written, and what kind of reading or research the student undertook. See how well you can promote an open-ended conversation related to the topic of the paper and to language use.

You may wish to try out the Student-Teacher Conference Notes worksheet on page 33. After the conference, think about what you could do to ensure a productive portfolio conference that would be helpful and worthwhile to students.

The regular informal exchanges between teacher and student about portfolio content are obviously very important, but the more formal conferences that anchor a successful program are of equal if not greater importance. Conferences are evidence that both the teacher and the student take the portfolio collection seriously and that the usefulness of the portfolio depends on an ongoing analysis of it. By blocking out time to conduct at least four formal conferences with each student each year, the teacher demonstrates a commitment to the program and a genuine interest in each student's progress.

Conducting Portfolio Conferences

The conference should proceed as a friendly but clearly directed conversation between the student and the teacher. The focus of the conference should be on how the use of language serves the student's needs and interests. This focus translates, in the course of the conference, into helping each student reflect on why and how he or she reads and writes.

Teachers will want to discuss with students the quantity of recent reading and writing compared with that of previous time periods, the kinds of reading and writing that the student has done, and the student's purposes for reading and writing. (Build on discussions about texts and authors by recommending related reading.) Teachers will also want to discuss how the inclusions in the portfolio came to be and whether the pieces represent experiences and ideas the student has enjoyed and thinks are important. Teachers should let students know that the portfolio documents say something important about the individual student's life. In fact, a significant portion of the conference may be dedicated to learning about the student's interests. Here are a few examples of the types of statements that might elicit a helpful response:

- You seem to know a lot about deep-sea diving.
- Where did you learn all those details?
- Have you looked for books about them?
- Why don't you write something about them?

The student, too, should feel free to ask questions:

- Which pieces seem the best to the teacher and why?
- Is it always necessary to write for some audience?
- What if a writer wants an idea or thought to be vague—remain private, though written?
- How can a writer stop to use reference materials to find the right word and spell it correctly without losing the flow of expression?

Conferencing with Students *(continued)*

These examples show how the conference can provide powerful, effective opportunities to teach and to guide language development. The conference conversations between the teacher and the student should be as unique as the individual student who joins the teacher in this exchange.

Ideally, each student will look forward to the conference as a time when student and teacher pay close attention to what the student has done; how the student feels about that performance; and what the student's needs and goals are. Such conferences encourage students to accept responsibility for their own development.

The following guidelines will help the teacher make the most of portfolio conferences.

Conference Guidelines

- *Conferences should be conducted without interruption.* Plan creatively: Perhaps a volunteer assistant can manage the rest of the class during meetings. Or, assign to other students cooperative-learning activities or other work that does not disrupt your exchange with the student. It may be necessary to conduct the conference outside class time.

- *Keep the focus on the student.* Make the conference as much like an informal conversation as possible by asking questions that will emphasize student interests, attitudes toward reading and writing, favorite authors, and topics they enjoy reading about. Demonstrate that you care what the student thinks and likes. You can also show that you respect the way a student's individuality is manifested in language use.

- *Let the conversation develop naturally.* Be an active listener: Give full attention to what the student is saying. The student's contribution is likely to suggest a question or comment from you, resulting in a genuine and natural exchange. There may be opportunities to get back to questions the teacher had hoped to ask, but teachers should respect the course that the exchange takes and realize that some of their planned questions will need to be dropped. Good listening on the part of the teacher will help create successful conferences that address individual student interests and needs.

- *Be sincere but not judgmental.* Avoid evaluating or passing judgment on interests or aspects of the student's language use. On the other hand, try to avoid continually expressing approval and thereby creating a situation in which the student tries to respond in a way that will win favor: The conference will then lose its focus on the individual's language needs and development.

For many teachers, the time and planning that the conference demands constitute the most difficult aspect of portfolio assessment. Think about how you can use all the resources at your disposal, and don't forget to enlist students' help. Ask them to help you schedule meetings, and request their cooperation so that the system functions smoothly.

Questions will undoubtedly occur to you while reviewing the student's portfolio. It may be useful to have a few notes to remind you of things you would like to ask. Do not, however, approach a conference with a list that dictates the exchange with the student.

Conferencing with Students *(continued)*

Don't hesitate to use the conference as a means of getting to know the student better by learning about his or her interests, pastimes, concerns, and opinions. This can be time well spent, particularly if it demonstrates to the student that the various aspects of his or her life can be very closely connected to the use and development of language arts skills.

Shortly after the conference, the student can translate his or her notes to a worksheet like the goal-setting form on page 31, which will ask the student to elaborate on the objectives that have been established.

- ■ *Keep the conversation open and positive.* It is fine to ask questions that direct the focus back to the collection, as long as that leads in turn to a discussion of ideas and content, the process of reading and writing, and indications of the student's strengths and progress as a language user. In general, however, teachers should ask questions that promise to open up discussion, not shut it down. Phrase questions and comments so that they invite elaboration and explanation.

- ■ *Gear the conference toward goal setting.* Identify and come to an agreement about the goals and objectives the student will be attending to during the next time period.

- ■ *Limit the attention devoted to usage errors.* If the student needs to focus on mechanical or grammatical problems, suggest that over the next time period the student pay particular attention to these problems when editing and revising. Do not, however, turn the session into a catalogue of language errors encountered. Keep in mind that if there are four conferences and each one tactfully encourages a focus on just one or two examples of nonstandard mechanical usage, it is possible to eliminate from four to eight high-priority errors during the course of a school year.

- ■ *Keep joint notes with the student on the conference.* To keep a focus on the most important aspects of the conference, you and the student should use the *Student-Teacher Conference Notes* form. Frequently, student and teacher will record notes based on the same observation: For example, the student might write, "I like to use a lot of verbs at the beginning of my sentences, but maybe I use too many." And the teacher might write, "Let's watch to see how often Cody frontshifts sentence elements for emphasis." The student might write, "Look for a novel about the Civil War." The teacher might note, "Find a copy of *The Killer Angels* for Cody if possible." The model for conference notes in this guide allows the two participants to make notes on the same sheet, side by side; thus, notes on the same point will roughly correspond. The teacher and the student can even write at the same time if they can position the note sheet in a way that will facilitate this.

Keep in mind that conference notes frequently serve as a reference point for an action plan that is then more fully considered on the goal-setting worksheet.

Types of Student-Teacher Conferences

In addition to the scheduled conference, there are several other types of conferences that teachers can conduct as a part of portfolio assessment:

Conferencing with Students *(continued)*

GOAL CLARIFICATION CONFERENCES If a student appears to be having trouble using the portfolio system, a goal clarification conference can be scheduled. The meeting's focus should be to help the student clarify and articulate objectives so that work on the collection is directed and productive.

It is important that this session not be perceived as being overly critical of the student. Be supportive and positive about the collection; try to generate a discussion that will lead to clear goals for the student. These objectives can be articulated on a goal-setting worksheet, which the teacher can help the student fill out.

PUBLICATION STAFF CONFERENCES Students who are publishing pieces they write may frequently meet as teams or in staff conferences to select pieces from their portfolio. They may also discuss possible revisions of manuscripts they hope to publish. Teachers may enjoy observing and even participating in these but should let students direct them as much as possible.

Other class projects and collaborative activities can generate similar student conferences that may involve portfolio collections.

INFORMAL OR ROVING CONFERENCES In these conferences, teachers consult with students about their portfolios during impromptu sessions. For example, at any time a teacher might encounter a student with an important and intriguing question, or spot confusion or a situation developing into frustration for a self-assessor. Often the situation calls for effective questioning and then good listening, just as in the regularly scheduled conferences.

Questions and Answers

The questions that follow are frequently asked by teachers who are thinking about instituting a portfolio management system.

- How can I make my students familiar and comfortable with the idea of creating portfolios?
- How often should my students work on their portfolios?
- How can I keep the portfolios from growing too bulky to manage and analyze effectively?
- Should I grade my students' portfolios?
- Who else, besides the student and me, should be allowed to see the portfolio?
- How can I protect against the possible negative effects of allowing a wide variety of persons to see students' portfolios?

How can I make my students comfortable with portfolios?

Teachers will, of course, want to begin by describing what portfolios are and what they are designed to accomplish. One way to help students visualize portfolios is to point out that some professionals keep portfolios:

- Artists usually keep portfolios to show prospective clients or employers what kind of work they can do. In a sense, an artist's studio is one big working portfolio, full of projects in various stages of completion.
- Photographers, architects, clothing designers, interior designers, and a host of other professionals keep portfolios full of samples of their work.
- Models carry portfolios of pictures showing them in a variety of styles and situations.
- Some writers keep portfolios of their work.
- People who invest their money in stocks and bonds call the collection of different investments they hold a portfolio.

Teachers can encourage students' interest by inviting to the classroom someone who can exhibit and explain a professional portfolio. Teachers might also show students an actual language arts portfolio created by a student in another class or school. Some teachers put together a portfolio of their own and use it as an example for their students.

After this or another introduction, you might share the following information with students:

- Explain what kinds of things will go into the portfolios and why. Students can choose what to include in their collections, but teachers can indicate that a few items will be required, including some records. Without introducing all the records to be used, teachers might show and explain basic forms, such as logs. If forms filled out by students are available, use them as examples.

Questions and Answers *(continued)*

- Stress that portfolios will be examined regularly. If the working portfolios will be available to parents or others, be sure to inform students. If you plan for others to see only show portfolios, this might be a good time to introduce this kind of portfolio.
- Show examples of holders that might be used, and explain where they will be kept. Students can be involved in making decisions about how and where portfolios will be housed.

How often should my students work on their portfolios?

The answer is "regularly and often." Teachers should schedule half-hour sessions weekly; ideally, there will be time almost every day when students can work on their collections. The Scheduling Plan on the next page shows activities that should occur regularly in your program.

How can I keep the portfolios from growing too bulky to manage and analyze effectively?

Because portfolios are intended to demonstrate students' products and processes over time, collections should be culled only when necessary. However, working portfolios can become simply too big, bulky, and clumsy to organize and analyze. If some students find their collections too unwieldy to work with, encourage them to try one of the following techniques:

- Cull older pieces except for those that stand as the best work examples. Put the removed contents into a separate holder and complete a *Description of Portfolio Contents* record. Explain on the record that the work consists of less-favored work, and have students take it home for parents to examine and/or save. Photocopies of later work that you consider more successful can be included as comparison.
- Close the whole collection, except for writing not yet completed, notes and records the student intends to use, and other idea files. Send the entire collection home with an explanation record and start a new portfolio.
- Cull from the collection one or more show portfolios for particular audiences, such as parents, other relatives, other teachers, administrators, or supervisors. After the show portfolio has been viewed, return it to the rest of the collection. Start a new portfolio, beginning with the ideas in progress.

Some teachers have their students prepare a larger decorated box to take home at the beginning of the school year. This container eventually holds banded groups of papers culled during the year. Students then have one repository for their entire portfolio collection, which they can keep indefinitely.

Questions and Answers *(continued)*

▶ SCHEDULING PLAN FOR PORTFOLIO ASSESSMENT

Activity	Frequency	The Student	The Teacher
Keeping logs	As reading, writing, and other language experiences are completed; daily if necessary	Makes the entries on the *Reading Record, Writing Record, Speaking and Listening Record,* and *Viewing Record*	Encourages the student to make regular entries and discusses with the student indications of progress, developing interests, etc.
Collecting writing samples, reactions to reading, entries that reflect on oral language	As drafts and reactions to reading become available; can be as often as daily	Selects materials to be included	Can select materials to be included; may require some inclusions
Keeping journal(s)	Ongoing basis; daily to at least once a week	Makes regular entries in one or more journals	Analyzes journal writing discreetly and confidentially
Adding notes, pictures, clippings, and other idea sources	Weekly or more often	Clips and collects ideas and adds them to appropriate place in the portfolio	Reacts to student's idea sources (every month or so); discusses with student how he or she will use them
Explaining, analyzing, evaluating inclusions	Weekly; not less than every other week	Uses forms for evaluating and organizing work to analyze and describe individual pieces included	Analyzes inclusions and student analysis of them at least four times a year—before conferences
Completing summary analyses	Monthly and always before conference	Completes a *Summary of Progress* record while comparing it with previously completed summary	Completes selected *Progress Reports* at least four times a year—before conferences, relying on student summaries and previously completed records
Conferencing—informal	Ongoing; ideally, at least once a week	Freely asks teacher for advice as often as needed; shares emerging observations with teacher	Makes an effort to observe student working on portfolio at least every two weeks and to discuss one or more specific new inclusions and analyses
Conferencing—formal	At least four times a year	Prepares for conference by completing summaries; discusses portfolio contents and analysis of them with teacher; devises new goals; takes joint notes	Prepares for conference with evaluative analyses; discusses portfolio contents and analysis with student; establishes new goals; takes joint notes
Preparing explanation of portfolio and analysis of it to a particular audience	As occasion for allowing other audiences access arises	Thoughtfully fills out the form *Description of Portfolio Contents*	Keeps student advised as to when other audiences might be looking at the student's collection and who the viewer(s) will be
Reacting to a fellow student's paper or portfolio	When it is requested by a "partner" or other classmate	Completes the *Peer Evaluation: Any Project* form	Encourages collaboration whenever possible

Should I grade my students' portfolios?

Teachers might be tempted to grade portfolios to let students know that they are accountable for their work; teachers may also feel that a grade legitimizes—or at least recognizes—the time and effort that goes into successful portfolio assessment. Finally, many parents, school supervisors, and administrators will expect the teacher to grade the portfolio. These reasons notwithstanding, most portfolio experts recommend that portfolios not be graded. Keep in mind that the collection will contain papers that have been graded. A grade for the collection as a whole, however, risks undermining the goals of portfolio management. Grading portfolios may encourage students to include only their "best" work, and that practice may convey the message that student self-assessment is not taken seriously. Think about it: How would you feel if someone decided to incorporate your journal entries, your collection of ideas that interest you, and other notes and informal jottings into a package that was being rated and given a grade?

Who, besides the student and me, should see the portfolio?

This question raises some of the same concerns as the issue of grading portfolios. Teachers may feel some responsibility to let parents, a supervisor, the principal, and fellow faculty members know how the program is proceeding and what it shows about the progress of individuals or of the class as a whole. It is important to balance the benefits of showing portfolios to outside audiences against the possible adverse effects—the risk of inhibiting students, diminishing their sense of ownership, or invading their privacy. Above all, the primary aims of portfolio assessment must be kept in mind.

Following are some suggestions for showing portfolios, with respect to the audience involved.

Another way to involve parents in portfolio management is to let students plan a workshop on portfolio management geared for parents and others who are interested. Or, as suggested earlier, have students cull their collections periodically and take the materials home for their parents to see.

PARENTS OR GUARDIANS Family members will almost certainly be viewing the portfolio in one form or another. If parents or other responsible adults are to view collections only on more formal occasions, such as back-to-school night or during unscheduled visits to the classroom, then students should be assisted in creating show portfolios. If, on the other hand, the teacher will show students' portfolios without the owners' knowledge or chance to review the contents beforehand, the teacher must tell students this at the beginning of the year. Warning students of these unscheduled viewings may qualify their sense of ownership; it can also intensify their audience awareness.

Questions and Answers *(continued)*

Again, if portfolios will be shown to other educators, students should be made aware of this before they start to build their collections.

SCHOOL SUPERVISORS AND PRINCIPALS Students' portfolios can demonstrate to fellow educators how youngsters develop as language users, thinkers, and people; they can also show the kind of learning that is taking place in the classroom. When working portfolios are shown, they are usually selected at random from those kept in the class, and the owner's identity is masked. Show portfolios are usually prepared specifically for this purpose. Whether the teacher uses working or show collections (assuming the state or school system does not mandate one) may depend partly on whether she or he thinks the audience will be able to appreciate that the working collections show process.

CLASSMATES Students may review their peers' portfolios as part of the program's assessment. Even if a particular program does not include a formal peer review stage, remind students that peers may see their collections—either in the process of collaborative work or peer review, or because a student does not respect the privacy of others.

NEXT YEAR'S TEACHERS At the end of the school year, teachers can help students create a show portfolio for their next teacher or teachers. These portfolios should demonstrate the student's growth during the year and the potential of his or her best efforts. They should also indicate the most recent goals established by the teacher and the student, so that the new teacher knows how the student sees his or her language skills developing over the next year.

Encourage students to include finished projects as well as earlier drafts. Discuss what kinds of logs should be included— or have students prepare a brief report showing how goals have been met. A fresh table of contents would be useful, as would an explanation of what the show collection includes and what its purpose is. Teachers may want to let students make copies of some papers that they would also like to take home.

THE STUDENTS THEMSELVES At the end of the school year, portfolio contents can be sent home for parents to see and save, if they wish. Before doing this, teachers may wish to have students prepare a starter portfolio of ideas, writing, plans for reading, and so on, for next year.

How can I protect against the possible negative effects of allowing a wide variety of persons to see students' portfolios?

Whatever special reporting the teacher does with portfolios, he or she needs to offset any possible adverse effects by keeping the primary aims for portfolio assessment in mind:

Questions and Answers *(continued)*

- The overall goal of the program is to develop students as language users. That goal should become the focus of joint student/teacher evaluation of the student's progress.
- Another important goal is for students to develop a habit of self-assessment. That is why the collections must be readily available to students.
- The emphasis should be on examining the process by looking at the product and the way it is produced. Each portfolio should be a working collection containing notes, drafts, and records of the evaluation of its contents.
- The activities assessed should integrate reading, writing, speaking and listening, and viewing and representing.
- The portfolio should be controlled and owned by the student.
- The collections should include reactions to and applications of a variety of text and writing types—with a variety of purposes involving different audiences.

Further Reading

Arter, Judith A., and Spandel, Vicki. (1992) NCME instructional module: Using portfolios in instruction and assessment. *Educational Measurement: Issues and Practice,* 11 (1), pp. 36–44.
Practical, sequenced steps to a portfolio approach are presented as a training model.

Bishop, Wendy, and Crossley, Gay Lynn. (1993) Not only assessment: Teachers talk about writing portfolios. *Journal of Teaching Writing,* 12 (1), pp. 33–55.
This article shows how using writing-portfolio evaluation changes the way that teachers think about their roles, students, and students' writing. (Whole issue is on portfolios.)

Brown, Sarah. (Spring 1994) Validation of curriculum: Creating a multi-level book as a portfolio and more. *Exercise Exchange,* 39 (2), pp. 29–32.
Project portfolios represent various stages of student growth and writing achievement, result in a published volume of student writing, and validate a curriculum.

Cirincione, Karen M., and Michael, Denise. (October 1994) Changing portfolio process: One journey toward authentic assessment. *Language arts,* 71 (6), pp. 411–418.
Describes how one teacher matched authentic assessment to the instruction in her classroom. (Whole issue is on portfolios.)

Farr, Roger, and Farr, Beverly. (1990) *Language Arts Portfolio Teacher's Manual.* Integrated Assessment System. San Antonio: The Psychological Corporation.
This manual includes descriptions of how to use, rate, and interpret responses to the Integrated Assessment System and several chapters on developing and using portfolios.

Farr, Roger, and Tone, Bruce. (1994) *Portfolio and performance assessment: Helping students evaluate their progress as readers and writers.* Fort Worth: Harcourt Brace College Publishers.
Portfolio assessment and the development of performance assessments is explained in detail with numerous practical suggestions, checklists, and model forms. Working portfolios are recommended to promote students' analysis of their own language use.

Galbraith, Marian, et al. (1994) *Using portfolios to negotiate a rhetorical community.* Report Series 3.10. Albany, New York: National Research Center on Literature Teaching and Learning.
Teacher narration and discussion cover what is required in the negotiation and mentoring involved in becoming a co-assessor with the student of the student's work.

Grady, Emily. (Fall 1992) *The portfolio approach to assessment.* Fastback Series. Bloomington, Indiana: Phi Delta Kappa.
This booklet tells how to use portfolios to assess a wide range of student performance.

Hesse, Douglas. (1993) Portfolios and public discourse: Beyond the academic/personal writing polarity. *Journal of Teaching Writing,* 12 (1), pp. 1–12.
In addition to the writing students do for academic discourse and personal purposes, another kind, public discourse, makes portfolios highly effective. (Whole issue is on portfolios.)

Hewitt, Geof. (1995) *A portfolio primer: Teaching, collecting, and assessing student writing.* Portsmouth, New Hampshire: Heinemann.
This manual on portfolio assessment covers grades 3–12 and a broad range of key considerations, with generous examples from actual portfolios.

Palmer, Barbara C., et al. (1994) *Developing cultural literacy through the writing process: Empowering all learners.* Des Moines: Allyn and Bacon.
Emphasizing cultural literacy, this book addresses each stage of the writing process and treats portfolio assessment. Numerous model activities expand the writer's knowledge base and develop critical thinking.

Porter, Carol, and Cleland, Janell. (1995) *The portfolio as a learning strategy.* Portsmouth, New Hampshire: Heinemann.
Learning strategies involving portfolios and developing self-assessors are described.

Robbins, Sarah, et al. (November 1994) Using portfolio reflections to re-form instructional programs and build curriculum. *English Journal,* 83 (7), pp. 71–78.
English teachers in two schools rely on portfolio assessment to redesign their curricula.

Tierney, Robert J.; Carter, Mark A.; and Desai, Laura E. (1991) *Portfolio assessment in the reading-writing classroom.* Norwood, Massachusetts: Christopher-Gordon.
This presentation covers all aspects of portfolio assessment, relying on research and descriptions of actual implementation.

Valencia, Sheila W., and Place, Nancy. (May 1994) Portfolios: A process for enhancing teaching and learning, *The Reading Teacher,* 47 (8), pp. 666–669.
Aspects of a Bellevue (Washington) project helped teachers use portfolios effectively.

Valencia, Sheila W. (ed.), et al. (1994) *Authentic reading assessment: Practices and possibilities.* Newark, Delaware: International Reading Association.
Case studies describe authentic assessment in and beyond the classroom. Programs at particular schools and in particular states are detailed.

Summary of Progress: Writing, Speaking, and Representing

Complete this form before sitting down with your teacher or a classmate to assess your overall progress, set goals, and discuss specific pieces of your work.

Grade _____ **School year** _____ **Date of summary** _____

▶ **What work have I produced so far this year?**

Writing:

Speaking:

Representing:

▶ **What project do I plan to work on next?**

Writing:

Speaking:

Representing:

▶ **What do I think of my progress?**

What about my work has improved?

What needs to be better?

▶ **Which pieces of work are my favorites and why?**

Summary of Progress: Writing, Speaking, and Representing *(continued)*

▶ **Which pieces of work need more revision, and what is needed?**

▶ **How has reading, listening, or viewing helped me in preparing for papers or other projects this year?**

▶ **What a classmate or the teacher thinks about my progress**

In writing—

In speaking—

In representing—

Summary of Progress: Reading, Listening, and Viewing

Complete this form before sitting down with your teacher or a classmate to assess your overall progress; set goals; and discuss specific works you have read, listened to, or watched.

Grade _____   **School year** _____   **Date of summary** _____

▶ **What have I read, listened to, or watched this year?**

Reading:

Listening:

Viewing:

▶ **What do I plan to read, listen to, or watch next?**

Reading:

Listening:

Viewing:

▶ **What do I think of my progress in understanding what I read, hear, or see?**

What about my work has improved?

What needs to be better?

▶ **Which things that I've read, listened to, or watched are my favorites and why?**

SELF-EVALUATION

Summary of Progress: Reading, Listening, and Viewing *(continued)*

▶ **What topics in what I've read, listened to, or watched would I like to explore further? How would I explore these topics?**

▶ **How has writing, speaking, or making media products helped me to become a better reader, listener, or viewer?**

▶ **What a classmate or the teacher thinks about my progress**

In reading—

In listening—

In viewing—

Self-Evaluation: Any Project

Grade _____   **School year** _____   **Date of these comments** _____

▶ **Title of work:** _____   **This is the** _____ **revision.**

The purpose of this work is—

The work was written or created for this audience:

These are the things I like best about the work:

These are the things about the work that do not satisfy me:

The most difficult things about writing or creating this work were—

Peer Evaluation: Any Project

Person whose work I am reviewing:

Title of work: **This is the**   **revision.**

This is why the work is (or is not) appropriate for its intended audience:

This work could be improved by adding or explaining these things:

This work could be improved by cutting or replacing these things:

This work could be improved if the following things were reordered:

These are goals that could be considered for the next or a similar project:

These are the comments of _____

[Sign here if your comments are about someone else's paper]

Self-Assessment Record

Use this form to evaluate specific pieces of your work, including papers, stories, oral reports, or video projects. Be sure to think carefully about your reasons for assigning ratings to each piece of work.

▶ **Ratings:**   Needs Improvement   Acceptable   Excellent
                    1   2   3   4   5

Title or description of paper or project:

Rating:

In deciding my rating, what strengths did I see in the paper or project?

What weaknesses did I see in the paper or project?

Title or description of paper or project:

Rating:

In deciding my rating, what strengths did I see in the paper or project?

What weaknesses did I see in the paper or project?

Title or description of paper or project:

Rating:

In deciding my rating, what strengths did I see in the paper or project?

What weaknesses did I see in the paper or project?

Goal-Setting for Reading, Writing, Speaking, Listening, Viewing, or Representing

▶ GOAL	▶ STEPS TO REACH GOAL	▶ REVIEW OF PROGRESS
Reading Goals		
Writing Goals		

Goal-Setting for Reading, Writing, Speaking, Listening, Viewing, or Representing *(continued)*

▶ GOAL	▶ STEPS TO REACH GOAL	▶ REVIEW OF PROGRESS
Speaking and Listening Goals		
Viewing and Representing Goals		

Student-Teacher Conference Notes

Name of Teacher _____

▶ **Student's notes**	▶ **Teacher's notes**

Table of Contents: Organization of Portfolio

Decide on the major categories for your portfolio. In the sections below, list the categories you have chosen. The works themselves may be papers, speech note cards, videotapes, multimedia products, or any work you and your teacher agree should be included. In choosing categories, consider organizing your work by topic, by genre (essays, poems, stories, and so on), by chronology (order work was completed), by level of difficulty (work that was less difficult, somewhat difficult, and difficult), or according to another plan.

Grade _____ **School year** _____

► WORK IN EACH SECTION	► WHY I PUT THIS WORK IN THIS SECTION
Section 1:	
title:	
title:	
title:	
title:	
title:	
Section 2:	
title:	
title:	
title:	
title:	
title:	
Section 3:	
title:	
title:	
title:	
title:	
title:	

Description of Portfolio Contents

Use this whenever you are preparing your portfolio for review by your teacher or another reader.

Grade _____ **School year** _____ **I began this portfolio on** _____

How it is organized:

_____

What I think it shows about my progress . . .

as a reader:

_____

as a writer:

_____

as a speaker:

_____

as a listener:

_____

as a viewer of media:

_____

as a maker of media products:

_____

as a critical thinker:

Description of Portfolio Contents *(continued)*

▶ **Examples of My Best Work**

The best things I have read are—	Why I liked them—
The best things I have written are—	Why I think they are best—
Other things in my portfolio that I hope you notice are— 1. 2. 3.	What they show—

TO PARENT OR GUARDIAN

The Portfolio: What Does It Show?

In the left column of the chart below, I have noted what I believe this portfolio shows about development in areas such as reading, writing, speaking, listening, and critical viewing. The right column notes where you can look for evidence of that development.

A prime objective in keeping portfolios is to develop in students a habit of analyzing and evaluating their work. This portfolio includes work that the student has collected over a period of time. The student has decided what to include but has been encouraged to include different types of writing, responses to reading, and evidence of other uses of language. Many of the writings included are accompanied by earlier drafts and plans that show how the work has evolved from a raw idea to a finished piece of writing. The inclusion of drafts is intended to reinforce to the student that using language entails a process of revision and refinement.

▶ I believe that this portfolio shows—	▶ To see evidence of this, please notice—

Teacher's signature_____

Response to the Portfolio

▶ Please answer any questions that seem important to you. Use the reverse side for any additional comments or questions.

Parent or Guardian _____ Date _____

What did you learn from the portfolio about your student's reading?

_____

_____

_____

What did you learn from the portfolio about your student's writing?

_____

_____

_____

Were you surprised by anything in the portfolio? Why?

_____

_____

_____

What do you think is the best thing in the portfolio? What do you like about it?

_____

_____

_____

Do you have questions about anything in the portfolio? What would you like to know more about?

_____

_____

_____

What does the portfolio tell you about your student's progress as a writer, reader, and thinker?

_____

_____

_____

Do you think keeping a portfolio has had an effect on your student as a reader or writer—or in another way? If so, what?

_____

_____

_____

Is there anything missing from the portfolio that you would have liked or had expected to see? If so, what?

_____

_____

_____

Student Awareness of Language as Process

Ratings:

1 = minimal progress	4 = more progress than expected
2 = less progress than expected	5 = outstanding progress
3 = some progress	

▶ Processing strategy	▶ Rating	▶ Comments
Reads, writes, listens, and speaks with a specific purpose; can articulate these purposes		
Tends to appraise what he or she knows about the topic; applies available background knowledge to the task		
Considers clues that indicate what can be learned or confirmed; thinks about or preplans expression		
Predicts what is coming next in text or oral presentation; considers what should come next (analyzes writer/ speaker purpose and audience expectation)		
Pictures the meaning being made by reading, writing, listening, and speaking as the process unfolds		
Challenges the ideas, concepts, and details presented to see if they are making sense or are appropriate		
Considers strategy adjustments needed in order to construct clear meaning		
Seeks aid or advice when strategies do not resolve inability to construct clear meaning		

Student Performance Graph

RATINGS: 10 = OUTSTANDING PERFORMANCE   8 = GOOD PERFORMANCE   6 = AVERAGE TO ABOVE-AVERAGE PERFORMANCE
4 = AVERAGE TO BELOW-AVERAGE PERFORMANCE   2 = WEAK PERFORMANCE

Rating	1st Grading Period	2nd Grading Period	3rd Grading Period	4th Grading Period	5th Grading Period	6th Grading Period	Comments
10							**• Attitude toward using language** How much overall progress has this student shown?
9							
8							
7							**★ Involvement in improvement**
6							
5							**✗ Amount/frequency of use**
4							
3							**✓ Effectiveness of use**
2							
1							

Key Considerations in Growth of Language Use. Place the appropriate symbol for each category below opposite the rating for each period. Connect the symbols with different colored lines to create a chart.

• Attitude toward using language
How much does student enjoy reading, writing, speaking, and listening?

★ Involvement in improvement
How inclined is student to self-assess, revise, and set new language-use goals?

✗ Amount/frequency of use
How often does the student read, write, and speak with a clear purpose?

✓ Effectiveness of use
How strong is student's control of language conventions, diction, and style?

SELF-EVALUATION

Reading Record

▶ **Ratings:** ✓✓✓✓ Terrific   ✓✓✓ Good   ✓✓ OK   ✓ I didn't like it.

▶ Month/ Day	▶ Title, author fiction or nonfiction	▶ Notes about the book	▶ Rating

Reading Inventory

▶ Questions and answers about my reading	▶ More about my answers
How much do I read?	What kinds of things do I read?
How much do I read outside of school/at home?	What kind of reading do I do there?
Do I like to read?	Why or why not?
Of things I have read, these are my favorites:	Why do I like them best?
What topics do I like to read about?	Why do I like reading about these topics?
Is anything about reading difficult for me? What?	Why do I think it is difficult?
Has reading helped my writing?	Why do I think so?
How important is reading?	Why do I think this?

SELF-EVALUATION

<table>
<tr><td>

Reading Skills and Strategies

</td></tr>
</table>

Title: _____   **Author:** _____

▶ **Before I Read**

What can I predict will happen in the selection or book based on illustrations, heads, charts, or maps?

_____

What is my purpose for reading (to interpret, to enjoy, to get information, to solve a problem, etc.)?

_____

What do I already know about the subject of this selection or book?

_____

How will I adjust my reading rate in order to better understand the selection or book? What kind of resources will I need as I read (dictionary, thesaurus, atlas, etc.)?

_____

▶ **While I Read**

How does what I already know connect with what I'm reading?

_____

What kinds of details do I find interesting? Why?

_____

What questions do I have? Do I need to adjust my predictions? Why?

_____

▶ **After I Read**

What is my reaction to the selection or book? Why?

_____

How were my predictions different from what I found? Why?

_____

Reading Skills and Strategies Evaluation Scale: Narration/Description

DIRECTIONS Circle 0, 1, 2, or 3 below to evaluate each item.

| **Evaluation Scale:** | 0 = Not at all | 2 = Some of the time |
| | 1 = I don't know | 3 = Most or all of the time |

BEFORE READING

1. Previewing the Text

- I determine the type of selection or book I am reading (biography, novel, short story, play, folk tale, myth, poem, or personal or descriptive essay). 0 1 2 3

- I examine the difficulty of vocabulary and decide on an appropriate reading rate. 0 1 2 3

2. Establishing a Purpose for Reading

- I identify my purpose for reading (to learn something new, to understand, to interpret, to enjoy, to solve problems). 0 1 2 3

3. Using Prior Knowledge

- I consider how my experiences might be connected with the text. 0 1 2 3

- I consider what I know about the author or the genre. 0 1 2 3

- I make predictions about what I will read. 0 1 2 3

DURING READING

1. Responding to the Text

- I think about how my experiences are related to what I'm reading. 0 1 2 3

- I take notes or use graphic organizers. 0 1 2 3

- I identify setting, characters or people, conflicts, and themes. 0 1 2 3

- I use context clues to help me determine meaning. 0 1 2 3

- I identify narrative and descriptive details (the sequence of events, sensory language, and so on). 0 1 2 3

- I make predictions about what will happen next in the text. 0 1 2 3

2. Monitoring Comprehension

- I re-read passages when my understanding breaks down. 0 1 2 3

- I read faster or more slowly based on my comprehension of the text. 0 1 2 3

Reading Skills and Strategies Evaluation Scale: Narration/Description *(continued)*

DIRECTIONS Circle 0, 1, 2, or 3 below to evaluate each item.

> **Evaluation Scale:**   0 = Not at all   2 = Some of the time
>   1 = I don't know   3 = Most or all of the time

AFTER READING

1. Responding to the Text

- I reflect on the meaning of what I have read and how the meaning is connected to my knowledge and experience. | 0 1 2 3

- I react to the selection or book and make my own interpretation. | 0 1 2 3

- I evaluate my predictions. | 0 1 2 3

- I discuss my thoughts about the selection or book with others. | 0 1 2 3

- I extend my reading by choosing another related selection or book to read. | 0 1 2 3

- I apply my reading to a paper or project. | 0 1 2 3

2. Using Study Skills

- I summarize, paraphrase, or outline the selection or book. | 0 1 2 3

- I can return to the text and scan for specific information. | 0 1 2 3

Additional Comments:

Reading Skills and Strategies Evaluation Scale: Exposition

DIRECTIONS Circle 0, 1, 2, or 3 below to evaluate each item.

Evaluation Scale:	0 = Not at all	2 = Some of the time
	1 = I don't know	3 = Most or all of the time

BEFORE READING

1. Previewing the Text

- I flip through the pages, looking at headings, illustrations, graphs, maps, charts, or other visuals.　　0　1　2　3

- I determine the type of selection or book I am reading (textbook, manual, informative book or article about science, history, geography, etc.).　　0　1　2　3

- I skim the text to examine the difficulty of vocabulary and decide on an appropriate reading rate.　　0　1　2　3

2. Establishing a Purpose for Reading

- I set a purpose for reading (to learn something new, to understand, to interpret, to solve problems, to enjoy).　　0　1　2　3

- I write down questions I want answered in the text (*who? what? where? when?* and *how?*).　　0　1　2　3

3. Using Prior Knowledge

- I reflect on what I already know about the topic.　　0　1　2　3

- I make predictions about what I will learn from the text and how the text will be organized.　　0　1　2　3

DURING READING

1. Responding to the Text

- I think about what I already know about the topic and how the text supports or contradicts my knowledge.　　0　1　2　3

- I identify main ideas and supporting details.　　0　1　2　3

- I take notes or use graphic organizers to keep track of facts or examples that support the main idea.　　0　1　2　3

- I use my understanding of common text structures to follow the text; when necessary, I use graphic organizers to help me sort out text structure.　　0　1　2　3

Reading Skills and Strategies Evaluation Scale:
Exposition *(continued)*

DIRECTIONS Circle 0, 1, 2, or 3 below to evaluate each item.

Evaluation Scale:	0 = Not at all	2 = Some of the time
	1 = I don't know	3 = Most or all of the time

1. **Responding to the Text** *(continued)*
   - I note all problems and solutions or causes and effects.

     0 1 2 3
   - I summarize or paraphrase sections of the text to confirm my understanding.

     0 1 2 3

2. **Monitoring Comprehension**
   - I re-read passages when my understanding breaks down.

     0 1 2 3
   - I read faster or slower based on my comprehension of the text.

     0 1 2 3

AFTER READING

1. **Responding to the Text**
   - I react to the text and sum up what I've learned.

     0 1 2 3
   - I evaluate the credibility of the source or text.

     0 1 2 3
   - I evaluate my predictions about the selection.

     0 1 2 3
   - I discuss my thoughts about the text with others.

     0 1 2 3
   - I extend my reading by choosing another related book, article, or other work to read.

     0 1 2 3
   - I apply my reading to a paper or project.

     0 1 2 3

2. **Using Study Skills**
   - I summarize, paraphrase, or outline the text's main ideas and supporting details.

     0 1 2 3
   - I return to the text and scan for specific information.

     0 1 2 3

Additional Comments:

Reading Skills and Strategies Evaluation Scale: Persuasion

DIRECTIONS Circle 0, 1, 2, or 3 below to evaluate each item.

Evaluation Scale:	0 = Not at all	2 = Some of the time
	1 = I don't know	3 = Most or all of the time

BEFORE READING

1. Previewing the Text

- I flip through the pages, looking at headings, illustrations, graphs, maps, charts, or other visuals.   0   1   2   3

- I determine the type of selection I am reading (editorial, review, article, advertisement, etc.).   0   1   2   3

- I skim the text to examine the difficulty of vocabulary and decide on an appropriate reading rate.   0   1   2   3

2. Establishing a Purpose for Reading

- I set a purpose for reading (to learn something new, to understand, to interpret, to be persuaded, to solve problems, to enjoy).   0   1   2   3

- I write down questions I want answered in the text (*who? what? where? when?* and *how?*).   0   1   2   3

3. Using Prior Knowledge

- I reflect on what I already know about the topic.   0   1   2   3

- I consider what my opinion on the topic might be.   0   1   2   3

- I reflect on what I already know about the author or publication.   0   1   2   3

- I make predictions about what I will learn from the text and what the author's opinion might be.   0   1   2   3

DURING READING

1. Responding to the Text

- I think about what I already know about the topic and how the text supports or contradicts my knowledge.   0   1   2   3

- I identify the author's position statement and supporting reasons and evidence.   0   1   2   3

- I distinguish between facts and opinions.   0   1   2   3

Reading Skills and Strategies Evaluation Scale: Persuasion *(continued)*

Evaluation Scale:	0 = Not at all	2 = Some of the time
	1 = I don't know	3 = Most or all of the time

Responding to the Text *(continued)*

- I identify emotional and logical appeals, loaded language, and other persuasive techniques.　　　0　1　2　3
- I can usually identify logical fallacies such as either-or reasoning, glittering generalities, and so on.　　　0　1　2　3
- I take notes or use graphic organizers to keep track of facts, examples, or appeals that support the author's position.　　　0　1　2　3
- I summarize or paraphrase sections of the text to confirm my understanding.　　　0　1　2　3

2. Monitoring Comprehension

- I re-read passages when my understanding breaks down.　　　0　1　2　3
- I read faster or slower based on my comprehension of the text.　　　0　1　2　3

AFTER READING

1. Responding to the Text

- I react to the text and formulate my own opinion.　　　0　1　2　3
- I summarize the author's purpose and point of view.　　　0　1　2　3
- I evaluate the credibility of the source or text.　　　0　1　2　3
- I evaluate my predictions about the text.　　　0　1　2　3
- I discuss my thoughts about the text with others.　　　0　1　2　3
- I extend my reading by choosing a related editorial or another work to read.　　　0　1　2　3
- I apply my reading to a paper or project.　　　0　1　2　3

2. Using Study Skills

- I summarize or outline the author's opinion and supporting details.　　　0　1　2　3
- I return to the text and scan for specific information and arguments.　　　0　1　2　3

Study Skills Inventory

▶ Questions and answers about my study skills	▶ More about my answers
How often do I study? Do I study at a special time and place?	How do I decide when and where to study?
Can I locate the introduction, table of contents, glossary, appendices, and index of a book?	How might these parts of a book help me study?
Do I preview or skim major sections of the text I'm reading?	How can previewing or skimming help me?
Do I review the maps, tables, and other graphic organizers in the texts that I study?	What help do these features provide?
Do I take note of typographical aids such as bullets, headings, and subheadings?	How do these features help my understanding?
Do I use a dictionary, encyclopedia, or other specialized reference material in my studying?	Why or why not?
Do I ask myself questions about the text as I read? Do I use any study questions provided in my textbooks?	Why is asking questions important?
Do I use study strategies such as SQ3R, writing summaries and paraphrases, or creating graphic organizers?	How do these strategies help me?

Study Skills Inventory *(continued)*

▶ Questions and answers about my study skills	▶ More about my answers
Do I practice making generalizations or drawing conclusions?	Why is formulating generalizations and conclusions helpful?
Do I distinguish between fact and opinion?	How important is knowing the difference between them?
Do I note causes and effects or problems and solutions in the texts I read?	Why is understanding these relationships helpful to my study?
Do I make the necessary adjustments in my studying based on my reading rate?	Why is my reading rate important in studying?
Do I study by using key terms, such as *compare, contrast, explain, analyze, describe, argue, define,* or *list*?	How would using these prompt words increase my comprehension?
Do I extend learning by looking at the marginal notes, footnotes, and bibliographies of the text?	What additional information would the footnotes and bibliographies supply?
Are my study habits successful?	Why or why not?

Progress in Reading

Ratings:	1 = minimal progress	4 = more progress than expected
	2 = less progress than expected	5 = outstanding progress
	3 = some progress	

Volume of reading	Rating	Comments
Compared with last progress report		
Amount student is reading during unscheduled school time		
Amount student is reading outside of school		
Has read from a variety of genres and sources such as diaries, journals, newspapers, electronic texts, and speeches		

Interests growing out of and promoting reading	Rating	Comments
Interest in some topics has intensified		
Has read texts on a variety of topics		
Is developing clear preferences in reading		
Shares ideas, stories from texts read		
Appears to be more questioning; turns to texts for answers		

Progress in Reading *(continued)*

Attitudes about reading	Rating	Comments
Reads assignments without resistance		
Talks about favorite books, stories, articles; cites texts read; reacts openly to what has been read in class		
Is actively involved in portfolio self-assessment of reading		
Has improved perception of self as a reader; demonstrates confidence with texts and ideas		

Applied comprehension	Rating	Comments
Relates reading to experience and background		
Reading appears to be promoting writing and speaking		
Expresses and shows appreciation for new ideas		

Reading strategies	Rating	Comments
Thinks of reading as a process		
Appears to read more fluently		
Has strategies to seek help if needed		
Has a growing lexicon/vocabulary		

Progress in Reading Skills

> **Ratings:**
>
> 1 = minimal progress   4 = more progress than expected
> 2 = less progress than expected   5 = outstanding progress
> 3 = some progress

Comprehension skills	Rating	Comments
Can identify main ideas and details		
After reading, can recall many details accurately		
Uses context clues to define difficult vocabulary		
Recognizes and understands common abbreviations, symbols, and acronyms		
Can identify correctly the antecedents of pronouns		
Can follow written instructions		
Can follow sequences of events		
Can identify and follow common text structures such as compare/contrast and cause/effect		
Recognizes common genres and can identify some distinguishing features of each		

Progress in Reading Skills *(continued)*

Interpretive skills	Rating	Comments
Student can make logical predictions		
Can connect own knowledge and experience to the text		
Uses context clues to decipher meaning		
Can interpret character traits and relationships in fiction		
Can understand implied cause-and-effect relationships, implied main ideas, and implied sequences of events		
Can make generalizations and draw conclusions about a text		
Can decipher the meaning of abstract words and/or multiple-meaning words		
Can interpret figurative language		
Can accurately summarize a text		
Reads with an understanding of literary concepts such as setting, mood, theme, and so on		
In nonfiction, can identify an author's purpose and point of view		
Can synthesize information from more than one source		

Progress in Reading Skills *(continued)*

Critical thinking skills	Rating	Comments
Can differentiate fact from opinion		
Can assess the credibility of an author		
Can recognize logical and emotional appeals and identify their purpose in a text		
Can recognize bias		
Can interpret persuasive and propaganda techniques and identify their purpose in a text		
Can detect fallacies in reasoning		
Can distinguish between relevant and irrelevant material in a text		

Writing Record

> **Ratings:** ✓✓✓✓ One of my best!   ✓✓ OK, but not my best
> ✓✓✓ Better if I revise it   ✓ I don't like this one.

▶ Month/ Day	▶ Title and type of writing	▶ Notes about this piece of writing	▶ Rating

Spelling Log

Word	My misspelling	How to remember correct spelling

Vocabulary Log

Put a circle around any of the words on your list that you often use in writing or speaking. Underline any of the words on your list that you frequently come across in reading.

> **Ratings:** ☆ = a word that you want to remember and use in writing or speaking
> + = a word you want to recognize when you come across it in reading

▶ Word	▶ Brief definition or synonym	▶ Context phrase or sentence	▶ Rating

Writing Inventory

▶ **Questions and answers about my writing**	▶ **More about my answers**
How often do I write?	What types of writing do I do?
Do I write outside of school/at home?	What kind of writing do I do there?
Do I like to write?	Why or why not?
Of the things I have written, I like these best:	Why do I like them best?
What topics do I like to write about?	Why do I like to write about these topics?
Is anything about writing difficult for me? What?	Why do I think it is difficult?
Does reading help me to be a better writer, or vice versa?	Why do I think this?
How important is learning to write well?	Why do I think this?

Evaluating Your Writing Process

Choose one paper from your portfolio. Track your writing process for that paper by writing brief answers to these questions. Keep the questions and your answers in your portfolio.

Title of paper _____

▶ **Prewriting**

   1. How did you decide on your subject?

   2. Did you use any of the prewriting techniques we have learned in class? Which ones? How did they work for you with this assignment?

   3. Did you plan the organization of your paper before you started writing? Why or why not?

   4. What did you like best about this stage of the assignment? What did you like least?

   5. About how much time did you spend on this stage of the writing process?

▶ **Writing**

   6. What did you find easiest about writing your draft?

   7. What did you find most difficult about writing your draft?

   8. What was your primary concern while writing the draft? Organization? Style? Development of ideas? Something else? Why?

   9. What did you like best about this stage of the writing process?

  10. About how much time did you spend writing your draft?

Evaluating Your Writing Process *(continued)*

▶ Evaluating and Revising

11. Did you receive feedback on your draft from anyone? If so, was the feedback helpful? Why or why not?

12. What did you think about your first draft? Why?

13. In this stage, did you make any major changes to your draft? Why or why not?

14. What did you like best about this stage of the writing process? What did you like least?

15. About how much time did you spend evaluating and revising your draft?

▶ Proofreading, Publishing, and Reflecting

16. How did you proofread and design the appearance of your paper?

17. Where did you publish your paper? If you published your paper by reading it aloud, who was your audience?

18. What did you like best about this stage of the writing process? What did you like least?

19. On which stage of the writing process did you spend the most time? How did spending this time affect the quality of your final paper?

20. What will you do differently the next time you write? What will you do the same way?

Assessing Your Writing Process: Evaluation Scale

Choose one paper from your portfolio, preferably one for which you have your prewriting notes and all your drafts. Use the chart below to analyze your writing process. Circle the numbers that most clearly indicate how well your writing process meets the stated criteria. The lowest possible total score is 5, the highest, 20.

1 = Does not achieve these criteria

2 = Made some effort to meet these criteria but with little success

3 = Made a serious effort to meet these criteria and was fairly successful

4 = Clearly meets these criteria

Title of paper _____

▶ STAGE IN WRITING PROCESS	▶ CRITERIA FOR EVALUATION	▶ RATING
Prewriting	■ Used prewriting techniques to find and limit subject and to gather details about subject ■ Organized details in a reasonable way	1 2 3 4
Writing	■ Got most of ideas down on paper in a rough draft	1 2 3 4
Revising	■ Did complete peer or self-evaluation ■ Found ways to improve content, organization, and style of rough draft ■ Revised by adding, cutting, replacing, and moving material	1 2 3 4
Proofreading	■ Corrected errors in spelling, grammar, usage, punctuation, capitalization, and manuscript form	1 2 3 4
Publishing and Reflecting	■ Produced a clean final copy in proper form ■ Shared the piece of writing with others ■ Reflected on the writing process and on the paper's strengths and weaknesses	1 2 3 4

Additional Comments:

Evaluating and Revising Your Draft

Read through your draft using the following five steps as a guide. Answer
each question fully and thoughtfully.

Title of paper _____

▶ **STEP 1: Thinking About Your Readers**

How do you want your readers to react to your paper?

Read through your paper quickly without stopping. Then, state what you think the readers' reactions
will be.

If the readers' reactions are likely to be different than the reaction you want, what do you need to
change in the paper?

▶ **STEP 2: Looking at Your Introduction**

Look closely at the introduction to your paper. What does the introduction do to capture the readers'
interest?

What do you like best about your introduction?

What do you like least about your introduction? What might you add, cut, replace, or reorder to
strengthen it?

Evaluating and Revising Your Draft (continued)

STEP 3: Looking at the Body

Read carefully through the body of your paper. What main points or ideas do you want your readers to understand?

Do you think the reader will consider the order of your ideas or points logical? Explain.

What examples of vivid, precise, or persuasive language do you find in the body of the essay?

Does this assignment call for examples and facts? If so, what examples and facts have you used?

Where might additional facts and examples be helpful?

Do any facts or examples seem unrelated or unnecessary? Why?

What might you add, cut, replace, or reorder to strengthen the body of the paper?

Evaluating and Revising Your Draft *(continued)*

▶ **STEP 4: Looking at the Conclusion**

Look closely at the conclusion of your paper. What does the conclusion do to bring the paper to a satisfactory close?

What do you like best about your conclusion?

What do you like least?

What might you add, cut, replace, or reorder to strengthen your conclusion?

▶ **STEP 5: Hearing How the Paper Sounds**

Read your paper aloud. Which sentences sound especially good to you?

Which sentences seem awkward, wordy, or unclear?

What words or phrases might you add, cut, replace, or reorder to strengthen those sentences?

Evaluating and Revising Checklist

Revise your paper until you can answer yes to each of the following questions. Add, cut, replace, or reorder material in your paper as necessary.

Title of paper _____

Content	Yes	No
Does the introduction grab the reader's interest?		
Is the introduction clear and logical?		
From the beginning of the paper, are the subject and purpose of the paper clear?		
Is the body of the paper well developed?		
Is each main point in the paper elaborated with facts, details, or other support?		
Is the paper free of unrelated or unnecessary ideas?		
Is the paper interesting?		
Does the paper end in a way that is satisfying to the reader?		
Does the paper achieve its purpose? (Before you answer, take a moment to recall the paper's purpose as clearly as possible.)		

Organization	Yes	No
Are the ideas and details arranged in a clear and logical order?		
Have transitions been used to make clear the relationships between sentences and paragraphs?		

Style	Yes	No
Is every sentence in the paper clear and smoothly written?		
Is the language of the paper appropriate for its audience and purpose?		
Have you avoided choppy and wordy sentences? Have you varied your sentence lengths and structures?		

Additional Notes:

Evaluating Content and Organization

Writer's name _____ **Title of paper** _____

▶**Introduction**

The best thing about the introduction is—

To improve the introduction, the writer might—

▶**Body**

The two best things about the body are—

The body's organization is or is not clear because—

To improve the body, the writer might—

▶**Conclusion**

The best thing about the conclusion is—

To improve the conclusion, the writer might—

▶**Overall Evaluation**

What does this writer do best of all?

Check the element that the writer should concentrate most on when revising.

_____ Interest Level _____ Style _____ Organization _____ Development of Ideas

Evaluating Audience and Purpose

Writer's name _____   Title of paper_____

▶ **STEP 1: Evaluating for Audience**

Who is the intended audience of the paper?

What information, ideas, or attitudes are they likely to have about the subject of the paper?

Has the writer taken the audience's knowledge, ideas, and attitudes into account? How can you tell?

Considering the nature of the audience, does the writer need to add material to the paper or delete material from the paper? If so, what?

▶ **STEP 2: Evaluating for Purpose**

What is the purpose of the paper?

What are some characteristics that papers with that purpose usually have?

Which of those characteristics does this paper have? Give examples.

Which of those characteristics (if any) are missing from this paper? What reasons might the writer have for ignoring those characteristics?

How successful is the writer in achieving his or her purpose? What might contribute to the writer's further success?

▶ **STEP 3: Overall Evaluation**

What is the most important thing the writer needs to do to be certain of achieving his or her purpose with this audience?

Revising: A Reader's Response

Writer's name _____ **Title of paper** _____

1. Which part of the paper did you find most interesting? Why? _____

   _____

   _____

2. Which part of the paper might the writer make more interesting? _____

   _____

   How would you suggest that the writer do this? _____

   _____

3. What is the writer's purpose? How can you tell? _____

   _____

   Do you think the writer is successful in achieving the purpose? Explain. _____

   _____

   _____

4. Are any parts of the paper difficult to read or understand? If so, which ones and why?

   _____

   _____

5. How would you assess the writer's editing and proofreading? Explain.

   _____

   _____

6. When the writer revises, is there anything that he or she definitely should not change?

   _____

   _____

7. Suggest two specific things the writer could do to improve the paper.

   _____

   _____

8. Tell the writer what he or she did well or what you will remember about this paper.

   _____

   _____

Revising: Four-Point Evaluation Form

Read the following list of criteria for good writing. Then, with these criteria in mind, read your classmate's paper. Finally, for each criterion, rate the piece of writing from 1 to 4.

1 = Does not achieve this standard

2 = Made some effort to meet this standard but with little success

3 = Made a serious effort to meet this standard and was fairly successful

4 = Clearly meets this standard

Be ready to discuss your evaluation with the writer and to make suggestions for revision.

Writer's name _____ Title of paper _____

Criteria for Evaluation	Rating			
■ The writing is interesting.	1	2	3	4
■ The writing achieves its purpose.	1	2	3	4
■ The writing contains enough details.	1	2	3	4
■ The writing does not contain unrelated ideas.	1	2	3	4
■ The ideas and details are arranged in an effective order.	1	2	3	4
■ The connections between ideas and between sentences are clear.	1	2	3	4
■ The writer's meaning is clear throughout.	1	2	3	4
■ The language fits the audience and purpose of the piece of writing.	1	2	3	4
■ The sentences read smoothly.	1	2	3	4
■ The paper is free (or almost free) of problems in grammar and usage.	1	2	3	4
■ The paper is free (or almost free) of problems in punctuation and capitalization.	1	2	3	4
■ The paper is free (or almost free) of problems in spelling and manuscript form.	1	2	3	4
Total:				

General Analytic Scale

The points possible for each of the twelve criteria listed in the chart may vary depending on the writing assignment that is being evaluated. Your teacher may give you the points possible for each category. Or, for some assignments, your teacher may give you the responsibility of deciding the points possible.

After you have filled out the **Points Possible** column, read the paper (your own or a classmate's) carefully and thoughtfully. Complete the **Points Given** column and tally the score.

Writer's name _____ **Title of paper** _____

CRITERIA FOR EVALUATION	Points Possible	Points Given
Content		
Is the writing interesting?		
Does the writing achieve its purpose?		
Are there enough details?		
Are the ideas related to the topic?		
Organization		
Are ideas and details arranged in an effective order?		
Are the connections between ideas, sentences, and paragraphs clear?		
Style		
Is the meaning of each sentence clear?		
Are the language and tone appropriate for the audience, topic, and purpose?		
Do sentences read smoothly?		
Grammar and Usage		
Is the paper relatively free of problems in grammar and usage?		
Punctuation, Capitalization, and Spelling		
Is the paper relatively free of problems in punctuation, capitalization, and spelling?		
Manuscript Form		
Is the paper relatively free of problems in manuscript form?		
Total Points		

Four-Point Analytic Scale: General

Circle the numbers that most clearly indicate how well the paper meets the stated criteria. Total the numbers circled. The lowest possible score is 15, the highest, 60.

1 = The paper clearly does not achieve this standard.

2 = The paper indicates that the writer has made some effort to meet this standard but with little success.

3 = The paper indicates that the writer has made a serious effort to meet this standard and that she/he has been fairly successful.

4 = The paper clearly meets this standard.

Writer's name _____ **Title of paper** _____

Content

■ The writing is likely to interest the intended audience.	1	2	3	4
■ The writing has a clear purpose and achieves that purpose.	1	2	3	4
■ The writing is unified and coherent.	1	2	3	4
■ The subject has been thoroughly explored and developed.	1	2	3	4
■ The writing does not contain unrelated or distracting details.	1	2	3	4

Organization

■ The writing has a clear structure.	1	2	3	4
■ Ideas and details are arranged in an effective and logical order.	1	2	3	4
■ The connections between and among ideas are clear.	1	2	3	4

Style

■ The language suits the topic, audience, purpose, and occasion.	1	2	3	4
■ The sentences are graceful and not awkward.	1	2	3	4
■ The paper avoids wordiness, stringiness, clichés, unnecessary jargon, mixed metaphors, and other stylistic pitfalls.	1	2	3	4
■ The writer's meaning is clear throughout.	1	2	3	4

Grammar, Usage, and Mechanics

■ The paper is relatively free of problems in grammar and usage.	1	2	3	4
■ The paper is relatively free of errors in spelling and mechanics.	1	2	3	4
■ The writer's respect for his or her audience is apparent in the manuscript form.	1	2	3	4

Total: _____

Open Analytic Scale

Writer's name _____ **Title of paper** _____

EVALUATION CRITERIA	Points Possible	Points Given
Content:	20 or ____	
Organization:	20 or ____	
Style:	20 or ____	
Grammar, Usage, Mechanics:	20 or ____	
Spelling and Manuscript Form:	20 or ____	
Total Points:	100	

Analytic Scale: A Personal Reflection

Read the personal reflection essay (your own or a classmate's) carefully and thoughtfully. Then, read each of the following criterion and complete the **Points Given** column. When you are finished, tally the score.

Writer's name _____   **Title of paper** _____

CRITERIA FOR EVALUATION	Points Possible	Points Given
Organization		
Are the events arranged in chronological order so that they are easy to follow? Are any flashbacks presented clearly?	5	
Does the writer use effective transitions to signal movements from one idea to the next?	5	
Content		
Does the introduction begin with an attention-grabbing quotation or anecdote?	5	
Does the writer provide enough background information to reveal what he or she was like prior to the experience? Does the writer also give the reader a clue to the importance of the experience?	10	
Does the narrative include vibrant narrative details?	10	
Does the narrative include vivid descriptive details, including sensory details and figurative language?	10	
Does the narrative include the writer's thoughts and feelings?	10	
Does the conclusion include a reflection of the significance of the experience?	10	
Style		
Is the tone and voice appropriate for the purpose and audience?	10	
Does the narrative use varied sentence structure to add variety?	10	
Grammar, Usage, Mechanics		
Is the narrative relatively free of problems in grammar and usage?	5	
Is the narrative relatively free of errors in spelling and mechanics?	5	
Does the narrative avoid errors in agreement?	5	
Total Points:	100	

Analytic Scale: A Comparison-Contrast Essay

Use the chart below to evaluate a comparison-contrast article. Circle the numbers that most clearly indicate how well the article meets the stated criteria. The lowest possible total score is 12, the highest, 48.

1 = Does not achieve this standard

2 = Makes an effort to meet this standard but with minimal success

3 = Makes a serious effort to meet this standard and is fairly successful

4 = Clearly meets this standard

Writer's name _____ **Title of paper** _____

▶ WRITING ELEMENT	▶ CRITERIA FOR EVALUATION	▶ RATING			
▶ **Organization**	▪ Details are arranged using a block or point-by-point method.	1	2	3	4
	▪ The writer uses transitional words and phrases to connect and clarify ideas.	1	2	3	4
	▪ The essay's organization is easy to follow and understand.	1	2	3	4
▶ **Content**	▪ The introduction grabs the reader's attention and clearly states the thesis.	1	2	3	4
	▪ The introduction clearly explains any necessary background information.	1	2	3	4
	▪ The body paragraphs clearly explain how the two subjects' relevant features are similar or different, or both.	1	2	3	4
	▪ The essay includes specific details that support the key points.	1	2	3	4
	▪ The conclusion summarizes the information and restates the thesis.	1	2	3	4
▶ **Style**	▪ The essay avoids worn-out adverbs.	1	2	3	4
	▪ The writer's tone is appropriate for an informative purpose.	1	2	3	4
▶ **Grammar, Usage, and Mechanics**	▪ The essay is relatively free of errors in grammar, usage, and mechanics.	1	2	3	4
	▪ The essay correctly uses modifiers that show degrees of comparison.	1	2	3	4
	Total Points:				

Analytic Scale: A Cause-and-Effect Explanation

Evaluate a cause-and-effect explanation by determining how well the essay
meets the following criteria. Total the numbers in the **Points Given** column to
determine an overall score.

Writer's name _____ Title of paper _____

CRITERIA FOR EVALUATION	Points Possible	Points Given
Organization ■ Causes or effects are arranged in chronological order or order of importance. ■ The organization is clear and easy to follow.	30 *or* ——	
Content ■ The introduction grabs readers' attention and prepares them for the explanations that follow. ■ The body paragraphs clearly explain the causes or effects of the topic. ■ The causes or effects are supported by fully elaborated evidence. ■ The conclusion restates the thesis.	40 *or* ——	
Style ■ The essay contains a variety of sentence structures and varied sentence beginnings. ■ The essay's diction and tone are appropriate for the audience and purpose.	15 *or* ——	
Grammar, Usage, and Mechanics ■ The essay is relatively free of problems in grammar, usage, spelling, and mechanics. ■ The essay avoids dangling modifiers.	15 *or* ——	
Total Points:	100	

Analytic Scale: A Problem-Analysis Essay

Evaluate a problem-analysis essay by determining how well the essay meets the following criteria. Total the numbers in the **Points Given** column to determine an overall score.

Writer's name _____ **Title of paper** _____

CRITERIA FOR EVALUATION	Points Possible	Points Given
Organization ■ The key points in the analysis are arranged so that they follow a logical progression. ■ The organization is clear and easy to follow.	30 *or* _____	
Content ■ The introduction creates interest, and, in a clear, concise thesis statement, outlines the problem to be analyzed. ■ The body paragraphs explain the impact of the problem on readers and fully analyze the problem. ■ Information is supported by facts, examples, statistics, or statements from experts. ■ The conclusion restates the problem and reminds readers of why it should matter to them.	40 *or* _____	
Style ■ The essay is concisely written and is free of redundant or flabby phrases and clauses. ■ The essay's tone is appropriate for its audience, occasion, and purpose.	15 *or* _____	
Grammar, Usage, and Mechanics ■ The essay is relatively free of problems in grammar, usage, spelling, and mechanics. ■ The essay avoids fragments.	15 *or* _____	
Total Points:	100	

Analytic Scale: A Literary Analysis

Rate how well the analysis of a short story meets the following criteria on a scale of 1 to 5, with 1 being the lowest rating and 5 being the highest. When you are finished, add the numbers to calculate a total score. The lowest possible score is 12, the highest, 60.

Writer's name _____ **Title of paper** _____

Criteria for Evaluation: **Rating (1 to 5):**

1. The essay opens with an interesting comment or observation.   _____

2. The writer provides the author's name, the title of the short story, and any relevant background information.   _____

3. The writer states the main idea of the analysis in a clear thesis statement.   _____

4. The writer summarizes, paraphrases, or quotes literary evidence from the short story.   _____

5. The writer fully explains how the evidence supports the thesis.   _____

6. The writer concludes his or her analysis by summarizing the thesis and the major points.   _____

7. The writer organizes his or her ideas in chronological order or by order of importance.   _____

8. The writer's tone is objective and formal; the writer's voice shows respect for the subject and the audience.   _____

9. The writer introduces quotations so the transitions between the writer's words and the words of others are clear.   _____

10. The analysis is relatively free of problems in grammar, usage, spelling, and mechanics.   _____

11. The writer uses varied sentence structure, including complex sentences.   _____

12. The writer uses quotation marks correctly.   _____

                                                      Total: _____

Analytic Scale: A Research Paper

Use the following questions to evaluate a research paper. Read the paper carefully. Then, award points for each criterion based on the number of points possible. Finally, add the points in the **Points Given** column.

Writer's name _____   **Title of paper** _____

CRITERIA FOR EVALUATION	Points Possible	Points Given
■ Does the paper have an informative title?	5	
■ Does the writer offer an attention-getting introduction?	5	
■ Does the writer include a clear thesis statement?	10	
■ Does the writer use primary and secondary sources to provide adequate and varied support for the thesis statement?	10	
■ Does the writer fully elaborate upon the support?	10	
■ Does the writer document the sources within the paper using correctly formatted parenthetical citations?	10	
■ Does the conclusion remind readers of the thesis and leave them with an unusual insight or question to ponder?	5	
■ Does the writer include a correctly-formatted Works Cited list?	10	
■ Is the organization of the paper easy to follow?	5	
■ Does the paper introduce quotations smoothly?	5	
■ Is the writer's tone appropriate for the audience and purpose?	5	
■ Does the writer use a variety of sentence lengths?	5	
■ Is the paper relatively free of errors in grammar and usage?	5	
■ Is the paper relatively free of errors in spelling and mechanics?	5	
■ Does the paper avoid misplaced modifiers?	5	
Total Points:	100	

Analytic Scale: A Persuasive Essay

Circle the numbers on the scales that indicate how well the persuasive essay meets the stated criteria. Total the numbers circled. The lowest possible score is 15, the highest, 45.

Ratings:	1 = Does not meet this standard
	2 = Made some effort to meet this standard
	3 = Clearly meets this standard

Writer's name _____   **Title of paper** _____

Organization

- Reasons are arranged to show a logical progression of ideas.   1 2 3
- The paper's organization is clear and easy to follow.   1 2 3

Content

- The introduction begins by drawing readers into the issue.   1 2 3
- The introduction provides any necessary background information.   1 2 3
- The writer includes a clear opinion statement.   1 2 3
- The writer develops at least three reasons in separate body paragraphs to support his or her opinion.   1 2 3
- Reasons are supported by logical appeals in the form of facts, statistics, opinions, and so on.   1 2 3
- Reasons are supported by emotional appeals, including examples, anecdotes, and connotative language.   1 2 3
- The writer avoids using circular reasoning and other fallacies in logic.   1 2 3
- The conclusion restates the writer's opinion and summarizes the reasons or gives a call to action.   1 2 3

Style

- The writer's tone is appropriate for the audience and purpose.   1 2 3
- The writer's diction is appropriate for purpose and audience.   1 2 3
- The writer varies sentence structure to avoid repeated passive sentence constructions.   1 2 3

Grammar, Usage, and Mechanics

- The paper is relatively free of problems in grammar, usage, spelling, and mechanics.   1 2 3
- The paper avoids double negatives.   1 2 3

Analytic Scale: A Persuasive Brochure

Circle the numbers on the scales that indicate how well the persuasive brochure meets the criteria. Total the numbers circled. The lowest possible score is 14, the highest, 42.

Ratings:	1 = Does not meet this standard
	2 = Made some effort to meet this standard
	3 = Clearly meets this standard

Writer's name _____ **Title of paper** _____

Organization

- Sections are arranged in a logical order.   1 2 3
- The brochure's organization is clear and easy to follow.   1 2 3

Content

- The front panel opens with a catchy slogan to grab the reader's attention.   1 2 3
- The front panel identifies the product, service, or cause the brochure advertises.   1 2 3
- The front panel uses eye-catching visual elements that will appeal to the brochure's target audience.   1 2 3
- The inside spread includes sections that explain the primary idea.   1 2 3
- The inside spread includes section headings and emphasizes major points visually.   1 2 3
- The middle panel continues to draw readers into the brochure with persuasive graphics and text.   1 2 3
- The back panel provides necessary contact information and tells readers what action to take.   1 2 3

Style

- The brochure is creative and shows attention to layout and design elements such as color.   1 2 3
- The brochure's diction is persuasive and appropriate for the audience and purpose.   1 2 3
- The brochure avoids cliches.   1 2 3

Grammar, Usage, and Mechanics

- The brochure is relatively free of problems in grammar, usage, and mechanics.   1 2 3
- The brochure uses consistent verb tenses.   1 2 3

Total: _____

Record of Proofreading Corrections

Keeping a record of your mistakes can be helpful. For the next few writing assignments, list the errors you, your teacher, or your peers find in your work. If you faithfully use this kind of record, you'll find it easier to avoid troublesome errors.

Title _____

Date _____

Write sentences that contain errors in grammar or usage here.

Write corrections here.

_____   _____
_____   _____
_____   _____
_____   _____
_____   _____
_____   _____
_____   _____

Write sentences that contain errors in mechanics here.

Write corrections here.

_____   _____
_____   _____
_____   _____
_____   _____
_____   _____
_____   _____

Write misspelled words and corrections here.

_____ _____   _____ _____
_____ _____   _____ _____
_____ _____   _____ _____
_____ _____   _____ _____

Proofreading Checklist

Read through the paper and then mark the following statements either **T** for true or **F** for false. Return the paper and checklist to the writer. Give the writer time to locate and correct the errors. After the writer has done his or her best to correct the paper, offer to assist if your help is needed.

Writer's name _____   **Title of paper** _____

_____   **1.** The paper is neat.

_____   **2.** Each sentence begins with a capital letter.

_____   **3.** Each sentence ends with a period, question mark, or exclamation mark.

_____   **4.** Each sentence is complete. Each has a subject and a predicate and expresses a complete thought.

_____   **5.** Run-on sentences are avoided.

_____   **6.** A singular verb is used with each singular subject and a plural verb with each plural subject.

_____   **7.** Nominative case pronouns such as *I* and *we* are used for subjects; objective case pronouns such as *me* and *us* are used for objects.

_____   **8.** Singular pronouns are used to refer to singular nouns, and plural pronouns are used to refer to plural nouns.

_____   **9.** Indefinite pronoun references are avoided.

_____   **10.** Each word is spelled correctly.

_____   **11.** Frequently confused verbs, such as *lie/lay, sit/set*, and *rise/raise*, are used correctly.

_____   **12.** Other frequently confused words, such as *all ready/already, farther/further*, and *fewer/less* are used correctly.

_____   **13.** Misplaced or dangling modifiers are avoided.

_____   **14.** Double negatives are avoided.

_____   **15.** All proper nouns and proper adjectives are capitalized.

_____   **16.** Word endings such as *–s, –ing*, and *–ed* are included where they should be.

_____   **17.** No words have been accidentally left out.

_____   **18.** No words have been accidentally written twice.

_____   **19.** Each paragraph is indented.

_____   **20.** Apostrophes are used correctly with contractions and possessive nouns.

_____   **21.** Commas are used correctly.

_____   **22.** Dialogue is punctuated and capitalized correctly.

_____   **23.** Italics are used correctly.

_____   **24.** Citations are correctly formatted.

_____   **25.** Any correction that could not be rewritten or retyped is crossed out with a single line.

Multiple-Assignment Proofreading Record

DIRECTIONS: When your teacher returns a corrected writing assignment, write the title or topic on the appropriate vertical line at right. Under the topic, record the number of errors you made in each area. Use this sheet when you proofread your next assignment, taking care to check those areas in which you make frequent mistakes.

▶ **TITLE OR TOPIC OF ASSIGNMENT**

Type of Error										
Sentence Fragments										
Run-on Sentences										
Subject-Verb Agreement										
Pronoun Agreement										
Incorrect Pronoun Form										
Use of Double Negative										
Comparison of Adjectives and Adverbs										
Confusing Verbs										
Irregular Verbs										
Noun Plurals and Possessives										
Capitalization										
Spelling										
End Punctuation										
Apostrophes										
Confusing Words										
Quotation Marks and Italics										
Comma or Paired Commas										

SELF-EVALUATION

Self-Assessment Record

Ratings:	Needs Improvement		Acceptable		Excellent
	1	2	3	4	5

What I am judging (title or description)	What I like:	What I don't like:	Rating

Evaluating Presentation and Format

The presentation of your paper can enhance your message, making your text more accessible and pleasing to your reader. Use the following rating scale to evaluate the presentation of your own paper or a classmate's.

Ratings:	Needs Improvement		Acceptable		Excellent
	1	2	3	4	5

Rating   Presentation Criteria

_____ **1.** If handwritten, the slant of the letters is consistent, the letters are clearly formed, and spacing is uniform between words.
Comments:

_____ **2.** If word processed, there is appropriate and consistent use of boldface, italics, underlining, font and font sizes; no more than two or three different fonts are used. In addition, the font styles are not fussy, cluttered, or used inconsistently.
Comments:

_____ **3.** There is sufficient balance between the white space on the page (spacing, margins) and text. The intended reader to can easily focus on the text; pages are not cluttered or completely filled with text.
Comments:

_____ **4.** The use of a title, subheadings, page numbers, bullets, and other typographical aids make it easy for the reader to find and understand the information presented in the paper. All headings and bullets clarify the hierarchy of ideas.
Comments:

_____ **5.** There is an effective integration of text and illustrations, charts, graphs, maps, tables, and other graphics. There is clear alignment between the text and the visuals; the visuals clarify and support key points in the text.
Comments:

_____ **6.** If a Works Cited or Works Consulted list is used, the citations are complete and consistently follow the Modern Language Association (MLA) style or another style.
Comments:

Progress in Writing

▶ **Ratings:**   1 = minimal progress   4 = more progress than expected
                   2 = less progress than expected   5 = outstanding progress
                   3 = some progress

▶ Volume of Writing	▶ Rating	▶ Comments
Compared with last progress report		
Amount the student is writing during unscheduled school time		
Amount student is writing outside of school		
Writes in different genres		
Writes with a variety of purposes		
Writes for a variety of audiences		
▶ **Writing Process**	▶ **Rating**	▶ **Comments**
Has obvious purposes for writing; writes about interests and background		
Demonstrates audience awareness		
Plans written efforts when appropriate		
Revises work		
Self-assesses using his or her portfolio collection		

Progress in Writing *(continued)*

Writing Strategies	Rating	Comments
Focuses effectively on topics		
Organizes material effectively		
Handles details effectively		
Writes with clarity and directness		
Diction—uses words effectively; makes varied and purposeful choices		
Appreciates the beauty and impact of language		
Demonstrates variety in the development of ideas		
Uses a variety of sentence structures		
Is developing a personal style		

Writing Mechanics	Rating	Comments
Uses words accurately and precisely		
Follows conventions of grammar and usage		
Punctuates and constructs sentences correctly		
Spells correctly		

Progress in Writing Conventions

Ratings:	1 = continues to have a problem in this area
	2 = has made gains in correcting problem
	3 = student does this correctly

Sentence Formation	Rating
Writes complete sentences; avoids fragments, unless used purposefully	
Avoids run-on sentences	
Avoids misplaced or dangling modifiers	
Uses subordination and coordination correctly in sentences (does not connect unrelated clauses)	
Uses parallel structure	
Does not omit necessary words, phrases, or clauses	
Usage	
Uses correct subject/verb agreement	
Uses tense correctly and consistently	
Uses auxiliary verbs and inflected verbs correctly	
Pronouns agree with their antecedents	
Pronouns are correct in nominative, possessive, and objective cases	
Avoids indefinite pronoun reference	
Uses apostrophes correctly	
Avoids confusion of word groups (adjectives with adverbs, singular with plural)	
Avoids double negatives	
Avoids confusion of comparative and superlative degrees	
Avoids inappropriate homonyms	
Mechanics and Spelling	
Uses capitalization rules correctly	
Uses end punctuation correctly	
Uses internal punctuation correctly	
Uses and formats paragraphs appropriately	
Can spell common and advanced words	

Brief comments:

Creating a Guide for Evaluating Papers

Check off each step as the class completes the activity.

_____ **1.** The students read their papers aloud. No one comments until everyone has read.

_____ **2.** The students decide what the papers have in common that makes them good.

_____ **3.** The students list the four most important criteria in the form of complete sentences. Each sentence begins "A good paper has (or does) . . ."

_____ **4.** The students review the writing assignment to decide if they want to include additional criteria, and any new criteria are added to the list.

_____ **5.** Working independently, in pairs, or in peer groups, the students evaluate their papers using the criteria as a guide, indicating how successful their papers have been in achieving each goal (1 = Not at all successful, 2 = Somewhat successful, 3 = Almost totally successful, 4 = Totally successful).

As a final step, students might meet in small groups to ask peer advice on how to rewrite in order to achieve a four (4) on all criteria.

Additional Instructions or Comments:

Speaking and Listening Record

Use this record for both formal and informal speaking and listening experiences. Log at least one experience a week.

> **Ratings:** ✓✓✓✓ This was very important!   ✓✓ I learned a little.
>   ✓✓✓ Worth doing/remembering   ✓ I wasted my time.

Date:

What I said, heard, or saw:

Notes about why this experience was or was not important, interesting, or useful:

Rating:

Date:

What I said, heard, or saw:

Notes about why this experience was or was not important, interesting, or useful:

Rating:

Date:

What I said, heard, or saw:

Notes about why this experience was or was not important, interesting, or useful:

Rating:

Speaking Inventory

Questions and answers about my speaking	More about my answers
How do I feel about speaking to friends?	What do I like to discuss with them?
How do I feel about talking to adults?	Why do I feel this way?
How do I feel about reciting or speaking to the class?	Why do I feel this way?
What is the most difficult thing about speaking?	Why is it difficult?
What techniques have I learned to improve my speaking?	How do I use these techniques with friends or in class?

Listening Inventory

▸ Questions and answers about my listening	▸ More about my answers
What kinds of music do I like to listen to?	Why do I like them?
What TV shows and movies are my favorites?	What do I like about them?
How well do I listen in school?	How much do I learn by listening?
Do I listen carefully to what my friends say?	What do I learn from them?
When is it difficult for me to listen?	What makes it difficult?
How do I use the praise and suggestions of others to improve my skills?	How do I feel about getting praise or suggestions for improvement?

Evaluating Your Critical Listening

To evaluate your ability to listen critically, answer the following questions about an oral presentation you recently heard. Compare your answers with those of other classmates who also heard the presentation.

Speaker _____ **Type of presentation** _____

1. What was the speaker's purpose? _____

_____

2. What main points did the speaker make? _____

_____

_____

3. What examples, details, illustrations, or facts do you remember from the presentation? _____

_____

_____

_____

4. Explain why you think the speaker chose to use the examples, illustrations, or other things you listed in your answer to Question 3. Be specific about as many items as you can. _____

_____

_____

_____

5. How were the points in the presentation ordered—order of importance, logical order, or some other pattern? _____

Was the organization effective? Explain. _____

_____

_____

6. As the speaker spoke, were you able to draw conclusions and make predictions about what would come next? Were they accurate? Why or why not? _____

_____

_____

_____

Evaluating Your Critical Listening *(continued)*

7. As the speaker spoke, were you able to make connections to your own experience or prior knowledge? Why or why not? _____

_____

_____

8. Did you detect any bias in the speech? If so, what? _____

_____

_____

_____

9. What emotional appeals or other persuasive techniques did you hear? _____

_____

_____

_____

10. Why do you think the speaker was or was not credible or qualified to speak on this issue?

_____

_____

11. If visual aids were used, were they effective? Why or why not? _____

_____

_____

12. What did the speaker say that puzzled or bothered you? How did that affect how you reacted to the presentation? _____

_____

_____

13. What do you consider to be the strengths of the presentation? _____

_____

_____

14. Did you note any weaknesses? If so, what were they? _____

_____

_____

Evaluation Checklist for a Speech

Evaluation Scale: 1 = poor/none 3 = average 5 = excellent
2 = fair 4 = above average

Topic and Purpose
- _____ ■ Topic sufficiently limited
- _____ ■ Specific purpose established

Introduction
- _____ ■ Gets attention
- _____ ■ Makes purpose clear
- _____ ■ Gives needed information
- _____ ■ Relates topic to audience

Development
- _____ ■ Main points clearly and logically organized
- _____ ■ Effective transitions
- _____ ■ Enough supporting evidence
- _____ ■ Evidence is relevant to audience and purpose
- _____ ■ Evidence clearly presented
- _____ ■ Effective visual aids

Conclusion
- _____ ■ Emphasizes main points
- _____ ■ Provides note of finality
- _____ ■ Ends with high interest

Verbal Delivery
- _____ ■ Rate appropriate
- _____ ■ Volume appropriate
- _____ ■ Pronunciation correct
- _____ ■ Enunciation clear
- _____ ■ Stresses, emphasis appropriate
- _____ ■ Pauses appropriate
- _____ ■ Tone appropriate

Nonverbal Delivery
- _____ ■ Gestures appropriate
- _____ ■ Facial expressions appropriate
- _____ ■ Eye contact good
- _____ ■ Posture acceptable
- _____ ■ Other body language appropriate
- _____ ■ Nervousness under control

Use of Visual and Audio Aids
- _____ ■ Microphone handled smoothly
- _____ ■ All visual aids (videos, multimedia presentations, overhead transparencies, posters, slides) are clear and large enough for the audience to see
- _____ ■ All audio aids (cassette tapes, CDs, etc.) are clearly audible to audience
- _____ ■ All visual or audio aids enhance the presentation by clarifying a point or providing a memory aid for the audience; none are distracting or simply ornamental

Language
- _____ ■ Word choice appropriate
- _____ ■ Level of formality/informality appropriate to occasion

Overall Evaluation:

Evaluating a Speech

Answer the following questions about a speech given by one of your classmates or one you heard outside of school.

Speaker _____ **Speech Topic**_____

- What was the speaker's purpose?

- How did the speaker's introduction get your attention?

- What main points did the speaker make?

- What evidence did the speaker give to support his or her points?

- Describe the speaker's verbal delivery. Was it effective? Why or why not?

- Describe the speaker's body language. Was it effective? Why or why not?

- Describe any visual or audio aids the speaker used. Were they effective? Why or why not?

- Was the tone of the speech appropriate for the audience, purpose, and occasion? Why?

- How did the speaker establish his or her credibility or authoritativeness?

- What did you like best about this speech? Why?

- What suggestions would you give the speaker for how to improve the speech?

SELF-EVALUATION

Evaluating My Oral Presentation of a Literary Text

Subject of my presentation _____

▶ Questions about my oral presentations of literary texts	▶ My responses
■ What criteria did I use to select the text (personal interest, universal appeal, appealing theme, exciting story, etc.)?	
■ Was my choice of text appropriate for the various audiences (subject matter, level of difficulty, length)? ■ Why?	
■ After studying the text, what interpretation did I make? ■ Was it valid or appropriate? Why?	
■ Did I prepare an introduction that provided information about the text, its author, and any important background information?	
■ Did I prepare a script of the text with appropriate cuts and marks for emphasis?	
■ Did I practice my presentation? How did practicing help my delivery?	
■ How did I use verbal and nonverbal strategies such as pitch, tone of voice, emphasis, posture, eye contact, facial expressions, and gestures to support my interpretation of the text?	
■ Were my verbal and nonverbal strategies appropriate to the meaning of the text as well as to my purpose, audience, and occasion? Why or why not?	
■ How did I ensure that my delivery was clear and audible to everyone in my audience?	
■ What did I learn from this performance that can be used to improve my next presentation?	

Listening to an Oral Presentation of a Literary Text

Speaker's name _____ Subject of presentation _____

Questions about the presentation	My responses
■ Was the selection edited effectively to make it more suitable for oral presentation to an audience? Why do I think so?	
■ Did the speaker introduce the presentation with any background information or information about the author?	
■ How did the speaker use tone of voice, pitch, gestures, and facial expression to depict different characters?	
■ In what ways did the speaker use his or her own voice and tone to reflect the meaning and mood of the literary text?	
■ What vocal techniques did the speaker use to emphasize the rhyme or rhythm of the literary text?	

Questions about my active listening	My responses
■ As I listened, did I try to predict what events or descriptions were coming next? ■ What clues enabled me to do this? ■ If I did not do this, how would predictions have helped my listening?	
■ Did I create mental images of events or descriptions as I listened? ■ If so, how did this increase my understanding or appreciation? If not, how might this have helped my listening?	
■ What personal connections did I make with the text as the speaker spoke? ■ How did such connections help my understanding, especially of theme?	
■ Was I able to make eye contact with the speaker? ■ What nonverbal feedback did I give to the speaker?	

Evaluating Informative Oral Presentations

Speaker's name _____ Type of message _____

▶ Questions about the message	▶ My responses
■ Was the purpose of the message clear? ■ Why or why not?	
■ Did the message have an attention-getting introduction?	
■ Did the message seem appropriate to the audience's interests and level of knowledge? ■ Why or why not?	
■ Were the main ideas or major steps easy to identify? ■ Did they follow a logical pattern?	
■ Were the key points of the message supported by sufficient details and reliable data? ■ Why do you think so?	
■ Did the message contain precise language? ■ Were words specific and concrete? ■ Was the vocabulary appropriate to the audience?	
■ Were visuals or sounds used to reinforce key points of the message? ■ If so, were they effective? ■ How?	
■ Was the delivery of the message effective? ■ Did the speaker seem confident? ■ Were the speaker's facial expressions, gestures, and movements natural?	
■ What suggestions do you have for improving the message or the speaker's delivery?	

Evaluating Persuasive Oral Presentations

Speaker's name _____ Subject of presentation _____

▶ Questions about the message	▶ My responses
■ Did the introduction grab the attention of the audience? If so, how?	
■ Did the message seem appropriate to the interests, knowledge, and attitude of the audience? Explain.	
■ Did the speaker clearly state the specific purpose of the message? What was it?	
■ Were reasons and supporting evidence clearly stated? ■ Was the evidence credible? Why or why not?	
■ Were ethical or emotional appeals used to motivate the audience? Explain.	
■ Were opposing viewpoints presented and refuted with reasons and evidence? If so, how?	
■ Did the message contain precise language? ■ Were words specific and concrete? ■ Was the vocabulary appropriate to the audience?	
■ Were visuals or sounds used to reinforce key points of the message? ■ If so, were they effective? How?	
■ Was the delivery of the message effective? ■ Did the speaker seem confident? ■ Were the speaker's facial expressions, gestures, and movements natural?	
■ What suggestions do you have for improving the message or the speaker's delivery?	

Evaluating Interviewing Skills

Ratings:

| 1 (poor) | 2 | 3 (average) | 4 | 5 (superior) |

Questions about my preparations and interview	Rating	Comments: Examples and explanations
■ I contacted my interviewee well in advance, introduced myself, stated the purpose of my interview, and politely set up an interview date and time.		
■ I prepared questions in advance, both factual questions and open-ended questions, that enabled the interviewee to speak thoughtfully for several moments at a time.		
■ I took notes during the interview, jotting down key points precisely.		
■ I practiced active listening, listening especially for transition words (*next, then,* etc.) that would indicate how the interviewee's narrative or explanation was unfolding.		
■ I reflected as I listened, comparing what I was hearing with my own experiences or prior knowledge.		
■ I asked follow-up questions when I did not understand or when a point needed to be elaborated.		
■ I provided nonverbal feedback (eye contact, nodding of head, etc.).		
■ I reviewed and summarized my notes shortly after the interview.		

Evaluating Panel Discussions

Ratings:

| 1 (poor) | 2 | 3 (average) | 4 | 5 (superior) |

CRITERIA FOR EVALUATION	RATING	COMMENTS: Examples and explanations
Preparation • The issue to be discussed is clearly defined. • The participants' use of relevant details and evidence shows that they have analyzed the issue (and done research, if necessary) before the panel discussion.		
Participants' speaking skills and courtesy • Participants use an appropriate volume and tone of voice. • Participants do not interrupt one another. • Participants disagree with one another in a respectful and constructive way. • If appropriate, participants use logical, emotional, and ethical appeals to persuasively make their points. • In any question-and-answer session, participants respond to questions appropriately.		
Participants' listening skills • Participants take notes when others are speaking. • Participants use body language, ask relevant questions, and make appropriate comments to show the speaker that they are listening. • Participants demonstrate that they have listened to others by paraphrasing or summarizing the preceding speaker's response before delivering their own responses.		
Moderator's role • The moderator introduces the discussion. • The moderator ensures that everyone has a chance to participate. • The moderator keeps the discussion on track. • The moderator summarizes the major points made in the discussion. • The moderator keeps the question-and-answer session focused on brief questions and answers.		

Evaluating Group Discussions

Ratings:

| 1 (poor) | 2 | 3 (average) | 4 | 5 (superior) |

CRITERIA FOR EVALUATION	▶ RATING ▶	COMMENTS: Examples and explanations
Purpose ■ The group goal is clearly stated as a question to be answered or a problem to be solved. ■ Members of the group are prepared to explore the question or topic. ■ Members follow a discussion outline or create a more informal plan that breaks the topic or problem into subsections.		
Member participation ■ Each member contributes information and opinions. ■ Each member asks relevant questions of other members. ■ Members stay on task. ■ Members maintain eye contact with other members and speak audibly and clearly.		
Courtesy ■ Members pay close attention to one another. ■ Members do not interrupt one another. ■ Members express any disagreements politely.		
Outcome ■ The group produces an answer to the original question or problem. ■ The group's findings are based on information presented in the discussion. ■ The majority of the group members agree with the group's conclusion.		

Overall evaluation

What was the strongest contribution to the discussion?

What was the weakest contribution?

What communication skills should the group continue to work on?

Progress in Speaking

> **Ratings:**
>
> | | |
> |---|---|
> | 1 = minimal progress | 4 = more progress than expected |
> | 2 = less progress than expected | 5 = outstanding progress |
> | 3 = some progress | |

Speaking behaviors	Rating	Comments
Volunteers to recite in class or to contribute to class discussion		
Communicates effectively with classmates one on one		
Comments indicate keen audience awareness		
Contributions are on-topic and of interest		
Expresses self clearly and logically both in formal and informal speaking		
Uses details effectively when speaking		
Is developing effective control of voice		
Can be persuasive when talking		
Contributes orally to goals of smaller groups		

Progress in Listening

Ratings:
1 = minimal progress
2 = less progress than expected
3 = some progress
4 = more progress than expected
5 = outstanding progress

Listening behaviors	Rating	Comments
Can follow orally presented instruction		
Pays attention to in-class contributions of classmates		
Responds in conversation in a way that indicates comprehension		
Participates in alternating exchange of ideas during conversation		
Follows orally administered directions appropriately		
Listens with a purpose; can ignore distractions		
Can adjust type of listening (critical, reflective, empathetic, or aesthetic) to suit purpose and occasion		
Is developing preferences for particular listening experiences (music, theater, etc.)		

Progress in Oral Presentation of Literary Texts

Ratings:

1 = minimal progress	4 = more progress than expected
2 = less progress than expected	5 = outstanding progress
3 = some progress	

Presentation criteria	Rating	Comments
Makes appropriate selections of texts		
Prepares script with appropriate cuts and marks script for emphasis		
Prepares an informative and appropriate introduction of the text		
Practices presentation of oral interpretation		
Performs a valid interpretation of the text		
Uses verbal skills (pitch, tone of voice, emphasis) to communicate mood, meaning, and characterization		
Uses nonverbal skills (posture, eye contact, facial expressions, gestures) to communicate mood, meaning, and characterization		
Speaks clearly and audibly, with effective vocal variety		
Uses suggestions from others to improve personal performances		

TEACHER'S REPORT

Progress in Listening to Oral Presentations of Literary Texts

Ratings:

1 = minimal progress	4 = more progress than expected
2 = less progress than expected	5 = outstanding progress
3 = some progress	

Listening behaviors and perceptions	▶ Rating ▶	Comments
Listens to oral presentations actively		
Develops appreciation for spoken language		
Appreciates how nonverbal gestures and strategies enhance the spoken text		
Identifies the story line in narrative texts; makes predictions about what will come next		
Makes a personal connection with the literature; understands how this connection enhances his or her appreciation and understanding of literature		
Interprets themes; thinks about how oral performance reveals theme, mood, and characterization		
Recognizes and analyzes use of aesthetic language (figures of speech, imagery)		
Discusses how use of aesthetic language enhances literary texts		

Progress in Evaluating Oral Presentations of Informative and Persuasive Messages

Ratings:

1 = minimal progress	4 = more progress than expected
2 = less progress than expected	5 = outstanding progress
3 = some progress	

Listening behaviors	Rating	Comments
Examines the organizational structure of the message		
Evaluates the support offered for the key points in the message		
Examines the use of visual and audio aids in the message		
Evaluates the effectiveness of the language used in the message, including the precision of explanations and/or the use of emotional appeals and other persuasive techniques		
Evaluates the comprehensiveness and fairness of the message; notes striking omissions and evidence of bias		
Identifies strengths and weaknesses in the delivery of the message		
Evaluates impact of message on intended audience		

Progress in Evaluating Interviewing Skills

Ratings:

1 = minimal progress
2 = less progress than expected
3 = some progress

4 = more progress than expected
5 = outstanding progress

Behaviors and perceptions	Rating	Comments
Prepares appropriate questions to ask the interview subject		
Shows awareness of the types of questions (fact, open-ended, etc.) and their purposes		
Shows awareness of the types of listening skills and styles (critical, reflective, empathetic) that may be used in an interview		
Shows awareness of the importance of offering verbal and nonverbal feedback—for example, eye contact, nodding, and follow-up questions—during the interview.		
Shows awareness of interview conventions and courtesy (politely setting up the interview, asking permission to audiotape, sending a thank-you note, and so on)		
Understands the importance of note taking during the interview and of preparing a final summary		

Progress in Evaluating Panel Discussions

Ratings:	1 = minimal progress	4 = more progress than expected
	2 = less progress than expected	5 = outstanding progress
	3 = some progress	

Behaviors and perceptions	Rating	Comments
Identifies the topic to be discussed or the problem to be solved		
Evaluates participants' preparation for the panel discussion; notes whether they have analyzed the topic or problem and identified possible subissues or solutions beforehand		
Evaluates participants' volume and tone of voice for clarity and appropriateness		
Evaluates participants' courtesy		
Evaluates participants' attentiveness to other speakers as shown by note taking, body language, questions, and comments		
Evaluates the moderator's effectiveness in ensuring that everyone has a chance to participate		
Evaluates the moderator's success in keeping the discussion on track		
Evaluates the moderator's summary of the major points made in the discussion		

Progress in Evaluating Group Discussions

Ratings:	1 = minimal progress	4 = more progress than expected
	2 = less progress than expected	5 = outstanding progress
	3 = some progress	

Behaviors and perceptions	Rating	Comments
Identifies the group goal		
Evaluates how well the group seems to follow an orderly informal plan or a discussion outline		
Evaluates members' contributions to the discussion; notes whether each member contributes information and asks relevant questions of other members		
Evaluates whether members are engaged with the group; notes whether members maintain eye contact with one another and whether they speak loudly and clearly enough for everyone to understand		
Evaluates members' courtesy towards one another		
Assesses whether the group reaches its goal		
Assesses whether the group's answer is based on information presented in the discussion		
Assesses whether the majority of the members agree with the group's conclusion		

Viewing Record

Use this record for different types of television programs, Web sites, films, and videos. Log at least one viewing experience per week.

Ratings:	✓✓✓✓ This was very important!	✓✓ I learned a little.
	✓✓✓ Worth doing/remembering	✓ I wasted my time.

Date:

What I saw:

Notes about why this experience was or was not important, interesting, or useful:

Rating:

Date:

What I saw:

Notes about why this experience was or was not important, interesting, or useful:

Rating:

Date:

What I saw:

Notes about why this experience was or was not important, interesting, or useful:

Rating:

Viewing Inventory

▶ Questions and answers about my viewing	▶ More about my answers
What kinds of visual media do I use or prefer—television, film, Web, or another type?	What do I like about these kinds of media?
What kinds of television shows and movies do I prefer?	Why do I like them the best?
How much am I influenced by what I see? For example, how apt am I to purchase something I have seen advertised?	What associations do I make between the image I see and myself?
Who makes the TV shows, magazines, or videos I like best?	What do I think their purpose is?
Do I ever notice the way that different news media (TV, Web, radio) differ in reporting the same event?	Why do they differ?
Who is the target audience of the shows and other media I like? How do I know?	How would people outside this target audience interpret these shows or other media?
Do I evaluate visual or audio techniques (close shots, objects out of focus, music, voice-overs, etc.)?	How aware of these techniques am I as I watch?

Representing Inventory

▶ Questions and answers about my representing	▶ More about my answers
What visual media do I prefer to use?	What do I like about using these visual media?
Before beginning any project, do I think about which visual medium would best suit my purpose?	How do visual media differ? What are their individual strengths and weaknesses?
Do I continually consider my audience when creating visual media?	How do my final products show that I've thought about audience?
Do I consider fairness to others' points of view when creating visual media such as videos?	How do I ensure that information is presented fairly?
Do I think about how a viewer or reader will navigate through the visual media I make— particularly Web sites?	How do I ensure that my information is complete without being cluttered or disorganized?
Do I consider design elements such as color, line, graphics, images, and photos when using visual media?	How and why do I use design elements?
When using film or video, do I consider how the sound and picture will work together?	How do I ensure that the sound and images in my film or video complement each other?

Evaluating Multimedia Presentations

Ratings:

    1 (poor)   2   3 (average)   4   5 (superior)

CRITERIA FOR EVALUATION	RATING	COMMENTS: Explanations and examples
Content ■ The presenter states the purpose of the presentation at the beginning. ■ The presentation is interesting and informative. ■ All the visuals support the purpose. ■ The presentation is organized in an effective way.		
Delivery ■ The presenter speaks clearly and loudly enough to be heard by the entire audience. ■ The speaker gives the audience enough time to look at each visual. ■ The speaker faces the audience during most of the presentation, only looking away when pointing out something on the computer or video screen or focusing on another type of visual aid. ■ The speaker operates all equipment smoothly.		
Visuals ■ The visuals present essential and relevant information. ■ The visuals are easy to read and understand. ■ The speaker presents the visuals at the same time as the points they reinforce. ■ The visuals use color to make the information clearer and easier to understand. ■ Photos are clear and easy to see.		
Music/sound effects ■ The music sets a mood. ■ The sound effects go with the images. ■ The music or sound effects are not distracting.		

Evaluating Documentaries

DIRECTIONS: Circle a number in each row to evaluate the items.

▶ **Evaluation Scale:**   1 = Poorly done   3 = Average   5= Superior
                         2 = Has some flaws   4 = Good

I. CONTENT

- The documentary reveals a main or controlling idea.   1 2 3 4 5

- The documentary is accessible and engaging.   1 2 3 4 5

- The documentary makes a contribution to a field of knowledge or to the   1 2 3 4 5
  viewer's understanding.

- The documentary provides a variety of content—interviews, action sequences,   1 2 3 4 5
  graphs, still photos, and so on.

- The documentary presents its subject accurately and fairly.   1 2 3 4 5

- The documentary thoroughly explores all important aspects of the subject; if   1 2 3 4 5
  appropriate, there are details that show evidence of research, including
  interviews with experts and relevant facts, examples, and statistics.

- The audio and visual elements work together to create a unified point of view.   1 2 3 4 5

II. ORGANIZATION

- The beginning of the documentary introduces the subject and grabs your   1 2 3 4 5
  attention.

- Each scene gives new information.   1 2 3 4 5

- The sequence of scenes makes sense; if appropriate, the sequence of shots   1 2 3 4 5
  builds narrative suspense.

- The voice-over supplements the action and dialogue.   1 2 3 4 5

- The end of the documentary sums up the information presented and leaves   1 2 3 4 5
  you with a final impression.

III. TECHNICAL QUALITY

- The sound quality is audible and consistent.   1 2 3 4 5

- The music adds atmosphere without distracting from the action or dialogue.   1 2 3 4 5

- The framing of individual shots is thoughtful and interesting.   1 2 3 4 5

- The camera work is fluid and interesting—there are a number of different types   1 2 3 4 5
  of shots, but the camera doesn't unintentionally jump around, loose focus, or
  draw attention to itself.

- Transitions are used between shots; all transitions are effective and smooth.   1 2 3 4 5

- Lighting is used to enhance atmosphere.   1 2 3 4 5

Evaluating Reflective or Descriptive Videos

Ratings:

| 1 (poor) | 2 | 3 (average) | 4 | 5 (superior) |

Criteria for Evaluation	▶ Rating	▶ Comments: Explanations and examples
The video reflects a particular point of view.		
The video contains essential details of the place or experience being captured, including sensory details such as characteristic sounds and images that reveal texture.		
Spatial shots or shots that portray time sequences are logical and coherent; all sequences of shots make sense.		
A variety of shots and/or angles are used and transitions between shots are smooth.		
The shots combine to present a dominant impression or theme.		
Lighting and music are used to set a scene or mood or to capture a place's character.		
The voice-over corresponds to the images.		
The video is interesting or engaging.		
At the end of the video, the viewer is left with a vivid or complete final impression of the place or reflection.		

Evaluating a Film

Title of film _____

1. What genre is the film—action, drama, comedy, or another genre? What are the common characteristics of this genre?

2. Does the film seem like a typical example of this genre? Why or why not?

3. How are characters depicted? What details (dress, gestures, etc.) reveal what they are like?

4. Are the characters realistic, or "round"? Or are they one-dimensional stereotypes? Explain.

5. What is the plot? Does it build to a climax and then end in a satisfying way? Explain.

6. What is the setting—or settings? Does it create a mood or impression? Explain.

7. What is the theme or message of the film?

8. What types of shots (close-ups, long shots, etc.) are used and what effects do they have?

Evaluating a Film (continued)

9. Are there any special effects? Are they necessary to the plot and effectively done? Explain.

10. Is the movie told from a particular point of view—either a character's or narrator's? If so, what effect does the narration have on your response to the film?

11. How are sound and music used? Are they appropriate to each scene, or do they detract from the dialogue and action? Why?

12. How is lighting used? Does the use of light and shadow create a mood or atmosphere? Explain.

13. What do you think of the casting choices? Would other actors have created more believable characters? Why?

14. If the film is an adaptation of a novel or play, what changes have been made from the original? Why do you think these changes were made? What effect do they have?

15. What overall evaluation would you make of the film? Explain.

Evaluating a TV Drama or Sitcom

Title of series or show _____

1. What genre is the show? What are the characteristics of that genre?

2. What audience do you think it targets?

3. What is the main plot of the show? What are the subplots, or less important story lines?

4. What is the main setting of the show? How does the setting affect the plot? If there is more than one setting, how are the various settings balanced and for what purpose?

5. Who are the main characters on the show? Are they realistic, or "round," characters, or are they more one-dimensional stereotypes?

6. How do you respond to the characters? Do you identify with them?

7. Is the dialogue on the show believable and well written? Why or why not?

8. What is the theme of the show? Why do you think so?

9. What kinds of advertisements interrupt the show? Why do you think these ads are shown?

10. What is your overall assessment of the show? Why?

Evaluating Television News

Name of news program _____

1. Is the news program you are evaluating a national news program, a local news program, or a newsmagazine? How does its genre differ from the other two?

2. What story does it lead with? Is the story hard or soft news—does it appeal to the head or to the heart? Explain.

3. What proportion of the news stories are soft news, and what proportion are hard news? Do you think this is a good balance? Why or why not?

4. Who do you think is the target audience of the program? Why?

5. What is the length of the show? What is the average length of the individual stories?

6. Do you think the length of each story is sufficient for providing complete information? Why or why not?

7. Choose a particular news story and explain how it captures the viewer's attention. Does it use emotional appeals? If so, how?

Evaluating Television News *(continued)*

8. In the story you chose, whose point of view is represented? Is there another point of view that is left out? Explain.

9. What kind of visuals are used in the particular story you chose? Do they play upon your emotions?

10. Who reports the news? Do reporters in the field and outside experts interact with the anchors or not? If so, why do you think this is done?

11. What does the set look like? What effect does this appearance have?

12. What do the program's slogan, title logo, and opening music tell you about its tone and purpose?

13. What advertisements are shown in the commercials that interrupt the show? Why do you think they are the ones used?

14. How reliable do you think this news program is? Why do you think so?

15. What is your overall evaluation of the show?

Evaluating Graphics

DIRECTIONS: Circle a number in each row below to evaluate the items.

> **Evaluation Scale:**   1 = Poorly done   3 = Average   5 = Superior
> 2 = Has some flaws   4 = Good

I. PLANNING

- The graphic is an appropriate vehicle for communicating the information.   1 2 3 4 5

- The information is complete; there are no obvious omissions or misleading groupings.   1 2 3 4 5

- The graphic supports a point made in the essay, article, or presentation.   1 2 3 4 5

- The graphic is commented upon in text of the essay or article or in the speaker's presentation.   1 2 3 4 5

II. LABELS

- The graphic has a title.   1 2 3 4 5

- Labels are accurate and complete but not wordy.   1 2 3 4 5

- The graphic uses easy-to-read fonts and appropriate font sizes.   1 2 3 4 5

- The graphic has a key or legend.   1 2 3 4 5

- The key or legend is simple and clear.   1 2 3 4 5

- All source information is clearly identified.   1 2 3 4 5

III. DESIGN AND SPATIAL ORGANIZATION

- Different types of information are presented in different colors or textures.   1 2 3 4 5

- The movement in a flowchart is clear; arrows direct the reader's eye in a logical pattern.   1 2 3 4 5

- The vertical and horizontal axes of a bar or line graph are clearly labeled.   1 2 3 4 5

- The time measurements of a bar or line graph start with zero.   1 2 3 4 5

- All amounts being compared in the graphic are expressed in the same units of measure.   1 2 3 4 5

- The wedges of a pie chart are arranged in descending order of size.   1 2 3 4 5

Overall Evaluation:

Evaluating Print Advertising

1. Who made the ad and why?

2. What is the message of the ad? What values or beliefs does it represent (for example, the belief that beauty leads to happiness, etc.)?

3. Does the ad appeal to the reader's intellect by presenting valid, logical reasons? If so, what are they?

4. What persuasive techniques (bandwagon, testimonial, plain folks, loaded words, and so on) does the ad use to appeal to the reader's emotions and desires? Why are they effective (or ineffective)?

5. Does the ad use images to effectively appeal to the reader's emotions or senses? What are they? Why are they effective—or ineffective?

6. How does the ad use color, line, shape, or texture to catch the reader's attention and reinforce the message?

7. Does the ad have a catchy slogan? Is the slogan appropriate for the target audience? Explain.

8. Does the ad accurately represent its product, service, idea, or cause? Is it fair and complete?

9. What is your overall assessment of the ad's effectiveness? Why?

Evaluating Web Sites

Ratings:

1 (poor)	2	3 (average)	4	5 (superior)

CRITERIA FOR EVALUATION	RATING	COMMENTS: Examples and explanations
Clarity ■ The site is easy to navigate. ■ The site contains a clear index. ■ Hyperlinks are clearly distinguished from text. ■ Text is easy to read.		
Content ■ The site contains complete information. ■ The site contains accurate information. ■ The site is fair, not overly biased. ■ The site is authoritative; the site or its producer has credibility on the topic or issue. ■ The site's producer is clearly identified on the home page. ■ The content is current; the last revision date on the page is reasonably recent. ■ The site is stable—it likely will remain on the Web for some time.		
Design ■ Color is used effectively—one color is used consistently for each different element of the site (hyperlinks, headings, etc.). ■ Photos, graphics, or animation enhance the site without distracting the viewer. ■ Colors, graphics, and other design elements are used to unify all the pages of the site. ■ Visuals download quickly.		
Organization ■ Each page provides substantial information. ■ All closely related information is located on a single page. ■ The pages are not crowded with too much text.		

Progress in Viewing

> **Ratings:**   1 = minimal progress   2 = less progress than expected   3 = some progress
> 4 = more progress than expected   5 = outstanding progress

► Viewing perceptions and behaviors	► Rating	► Comments
Identifies the purpose of various media presentations (i.e., informative, advertising, entertainment shows)		
Analyzes credibility of programs viewed (who made it and why)		
Speculates about the target audience of a media message and identifies what techniques are used to address that audience		
Analyzes how different media present the same event differently (newspaper, television, Web) and speculates about why this is so		
Evaluates audio and visual techniques (special effects, camera angles, music, etc.) and their effects		
Draws conclusions and forms opinions about the purpose and effects of media messages		
Articulates reasons for personal preferences in TV and movie viewing		

Progress in Representing

Ratings: 1 = minimal progress   2 = less progress than expected   3 = some progress
4 = more progress than expected   5 = outstanding progress

Representing behaviors and perceptions	Rating	Comments
Chooses medium appropriate to his or her purpose		
Considers target audience and how to attract its members		
Provides accurate, complete information without disorganization or clutter		
Is attentive to point of view and bias; presents information fairly		
Uses color, line, graphics, images, and photos to attract attention and provide clear information		
Considers how a viewer or reader will navigate through the media product; the design of product reflects thinking about the ease of its use		
If the product is a film or video, uses sound and images to complement each other; product reflects student's awareness of effective expository or storytelling techniques		
Reflects on the strengths and weaknesses of the final product		

Progress in Evaluating Multimedia Presentations

Ratings: 1 = minimal progress   2 = less progress than expected   3 = some progress
4 = more progress than expected   5 = outstanding progress

Behaviors and perceptions	Rating	Comments
Identifies the purpose of the presentation		
Evaluates whether the presentation is informative and interesting		
Evaluates how well the visuals support the purpose of the presentation; can detect whether they are irrelevant or used solely for ornamentation		
Evaluates the clarity of the visuals		
Evaluates the organization of the presentation		
Evaluates the effectiveness and relevance of the music and/or sound effects		
Evaluates the presenter's delivery		

Progress in Evaluating Documentaries

Ratings: 1 = minimal progress   2 = less progress than expected   3 = some progress
4 = more progress than expected   5 = outstanding progress

Behaviors and perceptions	Rating	Comments
Identifies the topic and overall tone of the documentary		
Evaluates the documentary's camera work and editing; identifies the purpose or intended effect of certain shots and edits		
Evaluates the documentary's use of music and sound effects; assesses how well sound and image complement each other		
Evaluates the documentary's organization; assesses whether the sequences and transitions make sense and create interest		
Evaluates the documentary's use of lighting to create mood and to portray scenes clearly		
Evaluates the documentary's point of view and fairness		
Evaluates the documentary's thoroughness; can cite details that reveal the maker's knowledge and/or research		
Assesses the informativeness and entertainment value of the documentary		

Progress in Evaluating Reflective or Descriptive Videos

Ratings: 1 = minimal progress   2 = less progress than expected   3 = some progress
4 = more progress than expected   5 = outstanding progress

Behaviors and perceptions	Rating	Comments
Assesses whether the video reflects a particular point of view		
Recognizes essential details of the place or experience being captured; assesses the effectiveness of the filmmaker's presentation of such details		
Evaluates whether sequences and individual shots are effective and coherent; assesses whether transitions between shots are smooth and clear		
Evaluates lighting, sound, and music for effectiveness in setting a scene or clarifying events		
Assesses the effectiveness of the voice-over and notes whether it corresponds to the images		
Assesses whether the video creates a vivid or complete final impression of the place or reflection		
Forms an opinion about the video's creativity or craftsmanship		

Progress in Evaluating a Film

Ratings: 1 = minimal progress   2 = less progress than expected   3 = some progress
4 = more progress than expected   5 = outstanding progress

Behaviors and perceptions	Rating	Comments
Identifies the genre of the film and assesses how well it fits the characteristics of that genre		
Evaluates the characterization in the film		
Evaluates the plot of the film		
Assesses the setting of the film and how it contributes to mood		
Identifies a theme of the film and can offer support for his or her view		
Evaluates shots, pacing, special effects, lighting, and sound and explains their contributions to the film		
Evaluates casting and speculates about other choices		
If film is an adaptation of a literary work, student identifies changes and evaluates their purpose and effectiveness		
Is able to give an overall evaluation and offer support for his or her opinion		

Progress in Evaluating a Television Drama or Sitcom

▶ **Ratings:**   1 = minimal progress   2 = less progress than expected   3 = some progress

4 = more progress than expected   5 = outstanding progress

▶ Behaviors and perceptions	▶ Rating	▶ Comments
Identifies genre of show and can recall several characteristics of that genre		
Can thoughtfully speculate about target audience		
Identifies plot and subplot(s)		
Evaluates setting		
Evaluates characters; can distinguish complex characterization from stereotypes		
Evaluates dialogue		
Identifies theme and can provide support for answer		
Assesses what information the interrupting advertisements can provide about the audience and purpose of the show		
Can offer an overall assessment and provide support for this opinion		

Progress in Evaluating Television News

Ratings: 1 = minimal progress   2 = less progress than expected   3 = some progress
           4 = more progress than expected   5 = outstanding progress

Behaviors and perceptions	▶ Rating ▶	Comments
Can identify the genre of the news program and recall characteristics of that genre		
Can distinguish hard from soft news and evaluate how well the show balances them		
Can speculate about target audience and offer support for his or her ideas		
Evaluates completeness of individual stories		
Evaluates fairness of stories; notes whose point of view is adopted and whose is omitted		
Evaluates visuals and their possible emotional impact		
Assesses the show's anchors, set, slogan, and music; notes how all elements contribute to the purpose and tone of the show		
Assesses what information the interrupting advertisements can provide about the audience and purpose of the show		
Evaluates the overall reliability of the show and provides support for opinion		

Progress in Evaluating Graphics

▶ **Ratings:**   1 = minimal progress   2 = less progress than expected   3 = some progress
                    4 = more progress than expected   5 = outstanding progress

Behaviors and perceptions	▶ Rating	▶ Comments
Evaluates the suitability of the graphic to convey the information it contains		
Evaluates the completeness and clarity of the graphic; checks that there are no glaring omissions or misleading groupings		
Evaluates the completeness and clarity of the graphic's labels		
Evaluates the use of color or texture to highlight different kinds of information		
Evaluates the clarity and size of the fonts used in the graphic		
Identifies the graphic's key or legend and evaluates its clarity		
Checks to see that the time measurements of a bar or line graph start with zero		
Checks to see that all amounts being compared in the graphic are expressed in the same units		
Assesses the logic of the graphic's design		

TEACHER'S REPORT

Progress in Evaluating Print Advertising

Ratings: 1 = minimal progress   2 = less progress than expected   3 = some progress
4 = more progress than expected   5 = outstanding progress

Behaviors and perceptions	► Rating	► Comments
Identifies the purpose and target audience of the ad		
Identifies the values or beliefs implied by the ad, e.g. that success depends on beauty, etc.		
Identifies valid, logical reasons in the ad		
Identifies persuasive techniques and evaluates their appropriateness to the ad's target audience		
Evaluates the ad's use of color, line, and texture		
Evaluates the ad's use of images and their intended purpose		
Evaluates the clarity and effectiveness of the ad's design		
Evaluates the language used in the ad for clarity, interest, and appropriateness for the target audience		
Evaluates the fairness of the ad		

Progress in Evaluating Web Sites

> **Ratings:**   1 = minimal progress   2 = less progress than expected   3 = some progress
> 4 = more progress than expected   5 = outstanding progress

Behaviors and perceptions	Rating	Comments
Evaluates the site's ease of navigation		
Evaluates the completeness of the site's information		
Evaluates the accuracy of the site's information		
Identifies the site's producer and assesses his or her credibility		
Evaluates the site's organization		
Evaluates whether the site uses color effectively and consistently		
Evaluates the site's use of images, graphics, photos, and animation		
Evaluates the site's currency and stability		

Cooperative Learning Record

Use this record to track and evaluate your writing conferences with other students, your work in small groups, your group projects, and your teacher conferences.

▶ **Ratings:** ✓✓✓✓ This was very important!   ✓✓ I learned a little.
          ✓✓✓ Worth doing/remembering   ✓ I wasted my time.

Date:

What I said, heard, or learned:

Notes about why this experience was or was not important, interesting, or useful:

Rating:

Date:

What I said, heard, or learned:

Notes about why this experience was or was not important, interesting, or useful:

Rating:

Date:

What I said, heard, or learned:

Notes about why this experience was or was not important, interesting, or useful:

Rating:

Cooperative Learning Inventory

▶ Questions and answers about my cooperative learning	▶ More about my answers
How do I feel about my role in the group?	What do I feel this way?
How much responsibility do I assume?	Do I like doing this? Why or why not?
How much do I participate in the group?	What do others learn from me?
How well do I stay on task?	What do I learn from others?
What is the most difficult thing about cooperative learning?	Why is it difficult?
What do I like about working cooperatively with others?	How might I use cooperative learning skills outside of school?

Evaluating Cooperative Learning

Use these questions to think about and evaluate your contributions to group activities.

1. What was your role in the group?

_____

2. What did you need to do to be useful in that role?

_____

_____

_____

3. Were you attentive and respectful to others in the group? What did you do to show these things?

_____

_____

_____

4. Were you able to stick to the subject or project at hand? Why or why not?

_____

_____

_____

5. What was your most important contribution to the group?

_____

_____

_____

6. What could you do to become a more effective group member?

_____

_____

_____

_____

_____

_____

_____

Evaluating Cooperative Learning

Use these questions to evaluate the contributions of another student in your group.

Group member: _____   **Group member's role in the group:** _____

1. Three words I would use to describe how the group member performed the role are
   _____

2. The member did the following things to work well with others (for example, asked questions to clarify the task, organized the agenda, or showed courtesy to other members):

   _____

   _____

   _____

   _____

   _____

3. The most important contribution the member made to the group was _____

   _____

   _____

   _____

   _____

   _____

4. This contribution was important to the group because _____

   _____

   _____

   _____

   _____

   _____

5. The group member could contribute more to the group if he or she _____

   _____

   _____

   _____

   _____

Evaluating Group Participation

Think about the work your small group did and then answer the following questions.

1. The students who participated in this group were _____

_____

_____

2. Our task was _____

_____

_____

_____

3. ▶ Circle your response to the following statements.

1 = Strongly Disagree   2 = Disagree Somewhat   3 = Agree   4 = Strongly Agree

The group did a good job of staying on task.	1	2	3	4
Every member of the group contributed to the group.	1	2	3	4
Each member of the group treated the other members of the group with respect and kindness.	1	2	3	4
The group felt that the task was worth accomplishing.	1	2	3	4
Each member of the group learned something from this experience.	1	2	3	4

4. What is the group's greatest strength? _____

_____

_____

_____

_____

_____

5. What does this group need to do to become more productive? _____

_____

_____

_____

_____

_____

TEACHER'S REPORT

Progress in Cooperative Learning

Ratings: 1 = minimal progress   2 = less progress than expected   3 = some progress
                4 = more progress than expected   5 = outstanding progress

Behaviors and perceptions	Rating	Comments
Actively participates in assigned role		
Communicates effectively with the group		
Assumes individual responsibility in learning		
Organizes work		
Focuses effectively on topic		
Demonstrates multiple problem-solving strategies		
Respects opinions, strengths, and weaknesses of others in group		
Demonstrates a positive attitude with the group		
Encourages others to participate		
Explains concepts; paraphrases and summarizes ideas		
Adds ideas and offers input		
Completes work		

Holistic Scale: Six Points

Score: 6 | **A score "6" paper has the following characteristics.**

All parts of the prompt are addressed with insight and control, and the writing is focused, clear, and well developed. All support is ample, specific, and relevant. The paper's organizational pattern enables a logical, coherent progression of ideas. The writer's engagement with the topic is clearly evident, as is his or her consideration of the intended audience's interest in and knowledge of the topic. The writer makes controlled and effective word choices and uses a natural, fresh voice; the paper is free of clichés and wooden phrasing. Sentence structure is varied, and fragments are used only when appropriate to writer's purpose. There are very few, if any, convention errors in mechanics, usage, and punctuation.

Score: 5 | **A score "5" paper has the following characteristics.**

The paper addresses all parts of the prompt with some degree of clarity and insight, although some minor lapses in coherence may be evident. The writer shows a consideration of purpose and audience, and the paper's organizational pattern is clear. All support is sufficient, specific, and relevant. When causal relationships are discussed, the writer makes all connections clear and explicit. The paper also exhibits a good command of language, including accurate and descriptive word choices. Sentence structure is varied and sentences are complete except when fragments are used for effect. The writer makes few errors in mechanics, usage, and spelling.

Score: 4 | **A score "4" paper has the following characteristics.**

For the most part, the paper is focused on the topic but may include irrelevant or loosely related material. The writer uses an appropriate organizational pattern, although some confusion in the logical progression of ideas may occur. The support includes specific details and precise word choices but is not ample nor evenly elaborated. In some responses, the writer demonstrates an awareness of audience, although this awareness is not exhibited consistently throughout the paper. Most sentences are complete, but there is little variation in sentence structure. There are few egregious errors in grammar, usage, and spelling.

Score: 3 | **A score "3" paper has the following characteristics.**

The paper addresses the topic in a reasonably focused way but may include irrelevant or loosely related material. The writer attempts to follow an organizational pattern, but may lapse into digressions or fail to provide transitions between ideas. The paper may also demonstrate little awareness of or connection to an audience. Some support, which may include specific

Holistic Scale: Six Points *(continued)*

details and relevant examples, is included, but development of such support is not consistent or substantial. Some "3" papers may appear to be somewhat elaborated summaries or lists of ideas. The writer's choice of words is generally adequate, but may be predictable or imprecise. The writer may vary his or her sentence structure very little, or not at all. Usually, however, the writer has a command of the conventions of written language.

Score: 2

A score "2" paper has the following characteristics.
The paper is generally responsive to the prompt but includes irrelevant or loosely related material. The paper may show few signs of an overall organizational strategy and few explicit transitions between ideas. Some papers may not exhibit a logical relationship between the main idea and subordinate ideas. Others may have an initial sense of purpose but then veer off-track. Support is generally unelaborated, consisting of lists or simple summary. The writer's choice of words is often imprecise or inappropriate, and sentence structure is unvaried or faulty. The writer may show limited knowledge of basic writing conventions.

Score: 1

A score "1" paper has the following characteristics.
The paper may address the prompt in only a minimal or tangential way. In addition, the paper may be highly fragmentary, often a listing of ideas with little development or organization of support. If any attempt to support or organize ideas is exhibited, a "1" paper is too short or skeletal to achieve a higher score. There is often no sense of audience or audience is badly misperceived. Coherence may be marred by vague or inappropriate word choice. Frequent errors in sentence structure and usage may also completely hinder the paper's readability. The writer may make blatant errors in grammar, usage, and mechanics.

Unscorable

The paper is unscorable because
- the response is not relevant to the prompt.
- the response is only a rewording of the prompt.
- the response contains an insufficient amount of writing to determine if it addresses the prompt.
- the response is a copy of a previously published work.
- the response is illegible, incomprehensible, or blank.

Holistic Scale: Six Points

Score: 6

A score "6" paper has the following characteristics.
All parts of the prompt are addressed with insight and control, and the writing is focused, well-developed, and forceful in arguing the writer's position. The writer maintains a consistent position throughout, and rebuts counterarguments with skill and purpose. All support is specific, relevant, and persuasive. The paper's organizational pattern demonstrates an awareness of the relative strength of the paper's arguments, ordering them in an obviously persuasive way. The paper also demonstrates the writer's engagement with the issue and his or her consideration of the readers' opinions and preconceptions about the issue. The writer makes controlled and effective word choices and uses a natural, fresh voice. Sentence structure is varied and fragments are only used when appropriate to writer's purpose. There are very few, if any, errors in grammar, usage, and mechanics.

Score: 5

A score "5" paper has the following characteristics.
The paper addresses all parts of the prompt with insight and attention to the persuasive task, although some minor lapses in coherence may be evident. The writer shows that he or she understands fundamental persuasive strategies and has considered audience, occasion, and tone. The paper's organizational pattern is clear and all support is sufficient, specific, relevant, and persuasive. The paper also exhibits a command of language, including precise, forceful, and vivid word choices. Sentence structure is varied and sentences are complete except when fragments are used for effect. The writer makes few errors in mechanics, usage, and spelling.

Score: 4

A score "4" paper has the following characteristics.
For the most part, the paper is focused on the persuasive task but may include some irrelevant or loosely related material. The writer uses an appropriate organizational pattern, although the persuasiveness of the argument may be undercut by occasional lapses in logic or coherence. The paper's support includes specific details, relevant examples, and precise word choices but is not ample nor evenly elaborated. In some responses, the writer demonstrates an awareness of audience, although this awareness may not be exhibited consistently throughout the paper. Most sentences are complete, but there is little variation in sentence structure. There are few egregious errors in mechanics, usage, and grammar.

Score: 3

A score "3" paper has the following characteristics.
The paper addresses the persuasive task in a reasonably focused way but may include irrelevant or loosely related material.

Holistic Scale: Six Points *(continued)*

The writer attempts to follow an organizational pattern, but may lapse into digressions or fail to provide transitions between ideas. The paper may also demonstrate little awareness of audience. Some support, which may include specific details and relevant examples, is included, but development of such support is not consistent or substantial. The writer's choice of words is generally adequate, but may be predictable or occasionally generic and imprecise. The writer may vary his or her sentence structure very little, or not at all. Usually, however, the writer shows a command of the conventions of grammar, usage, and mechanics.

Score: 2

A score "2" paper has the following characteristics.

The paper is generally responsive to the prompt but includes irrelevant or loosely related material. Many "2" papers will not offer a clear position on the issue nor pursue an explicitly persuasive strategy. The paper may show few signs of an overall organizational strategy and few clear transitions between ideas. Some papers may have an initial sense of purpose, audience, and writing strategy but then veer off-track. Support is generally unelaborated, consisting of lists or simple summary. The writer's choice of words is often imprecise or inappropriate, and sentence structure is unvaried or faulty. The writer may show limited knowledge of the basic conventions of grammar, usage, and mechanics.

Score: 1

A score "1" paper has the following characteristics.

The paper may only address the prompt in a minimal or tangential way. In addition, the paper may be highly fragmentary, often a listing of ideas with little development of support. Frequently, no organizational pattern is apparent. If any attempt to support or organize ideas is exhibited, a "1" paper is too short or skeletal to achieve a higher score. There is often no sense of audience or audience is badly misperceived. Inappropriate word choice and frequent errors in sentence structure may also completely hinder the paper's readability. The writer may make blatant errors in grammar, usage, and mechanics.

Unscorable

The paper is unscorable because
- the response is not relevant to the prompt.
- the response is only a rewording of the prompt.
- the response contains an insufficient amount of writing to determine if it addresses the prompt.
- the response is a copy of a previously published work.
- the response is illegible, incomprehensible, or blank.

Holistic Scale: Six Points

Score: 6 | **A score "6" paper has the following characteristics.**
The essay addresses and perceptively analyzes all the elements of the prompt. It is focused and thoughtful, reflecting insight into the literary work and a clear understanding of the form and purpose of literary elements. The essay has a clear thesis that is abundantly supported and illustrated by specific, relevant, and effectively elaborated evidence from the literary work. All ideas in the paper are organized in a logical and coherent way. The writer makes controlled and effective word choices and, although the tone is formal, the paper reveals a natural, fresh voice that is free of clichés and wooden phrasing. While the essay need not be flawless, its overall excellence convinces the reader of the writer's ability to read and write with clarity and skill. Few errors in grammar, usage, and mechanics occur.

Score: 5 | **A score "5" paper has the following characteristics.**
The essay addresses and accurately analyzes all the elements of the prompt, but slightly less thoroughly and accurately than the "6" essay. It reflects the writer's understanding of the literary work and reveals an understanding of literary elements and their contributions to the work's meaning. The essay has a clear thesis that is adequately supported and illustrated by specific, relevant and elaborated evidence from the literary work. The writer also demonstrates a maturity of style through his or her command of varied sentence structures, diction, and organization. The paper generally follows the conventions of grammar, mechanics, and usage. Stylistic flaws and minor errors may occur, but overall the essay demonstrates the writer's ability to write clearly.

Score: 4 | **A score "4" paper has the following characteristics.**
The essay addresses and analyzes some or all of elements of the prompt, but does so in a superficial manner. The essay contains a thesis vaguely supported by somewhat elaborated evidence from the literary work. However, the essay may also include irrelevant or loosely related material. The writing is sufficient to communicate the writer's thoughts, but it reveals little insight and only an adequate understanding of how literary elements contribute to the meaning of a literary work. The essay's sentence structure is mostly unvaried, predictable, and monotonous. Likewise, the writer's diction may be dull or slightly imprecise. A logical organizational pattern is apparent, although some lapses may occur. The essay generally follows the conventions of writing although there are lapses.

Holistic Scale: Six Points (continued)

Score: 3

A score "3" paper has the following characteristics.
The essay generally addresses the prompt but may include irrelevant or loosely related material. A thesis and some supporting evidence from the literary work are present, but neither is strong or convincing. Often "3" essays paraphrase rather than analyze; they may appear to be somewhat elaborated summaries or lists of ideas. Organization and word choice are generally adequate, but may be predictable or basic. The writer may vary his or her sentence structure very little, or not at all. Usually, however, the writer has a command of writing conventions.

Score: 2

A score "2" paper has the following characteristics.
The essay addresses the prompt but demonstrates an incomplete understanding of what it requires. It may indicate a serious misreading of the prompt or the literary work, or both. There is no discernible thesis, or the controlling idea bears little connection to subordinate ideas or supporting details. Some papers may have an initial sense of purpose but then veer off-track. Development of support is inadequate or illogical, often consisting of weak paraphrases of the work. Support may also consist of mostly unelaborated lists. The writer's choice of words is often imprecise or inappropriate. In addition, sentence structure is unvaried or faulty. The writer may show limited knowledge of the basic conventions of grammar, usage, and mechanics.

Score: 1

A score "1" paper has the following characteristics.
The writer shows little understanding of the prompt, the literary work, or the nature of literary analysis. In addition, the paper may be highly fragmentary, often a listing of ideas with little development or organization of support. If any attempt to support or organize ideas is exhibited, a "1" paper is too short or skeletal to achieve a higher score. Inappropriate word choice and frequent errors in sentence structure may completely hinder the paper's readability. The writer may also make blatant errors in grammar, usage, and mechanics.

Unscorable

The paper is unscorable because
- the response is not relevant to the prompt.
- the response is only a rewording of the prompt.
- the response contains an insufficient amount of writing to determine if it addresses the prompt.
- the response is a copy of a previously published work.
- the response is illegible, incomprehensible, or blank.

Holistic Scale: Four Points

Score Point 4

Responses that are organized, elaborated, and highly readable attempts to clarify, explain, or present information about the specified topic. Although a score "4" paper may exhibit a few inconsistencies, such inconsistencies are eclipsed by the overall quality, coherence, and thoughtfulness of the response.

- *The most characteristic trait of these responses is the ample and relevant support they contain;* all ideas are specific and well elaborated. Such responses are also characterized by most of the following:

  - ✓ *A unified organizational plan.* The responses have a clear organization and seem complete; if the writer employs more than one organizational strategy, all ideas still follow a logical progression. Minor inconsistencies may occur, but they do not detract from the overall order of the paper. In cases in which writers have run out of space, especially well-organized papers may still receive a "4."
  - ✓ *A marked command of written language.* These responses are fluent and clear; although some writers may not use all of the appropriate conventions of language, these responses are nevertheless quite skillfully written.
  - ✓ *Varied syntactic construction.* These responses contain compound and complex sentences.
  - ✓ *Concrete, vivid details.* All descriptions and explanations are communicated through thoughtful and effective word choices and expressions.
  - ✓ *Attention to all parts of the prompt.*

Score Point 3

Responses that are good efforts to clarify, explain, or present information about the specified topic. For the most part, a reader finds the paper clear, coherent, and reasonably elaborated.

- *The "3" category is composed of the following kinds of responses:*

  - ✓ *Papers that offer a great number of ideas, one of which is moderately elaborated, several of which are somewhat elaborated, or most of which are extended.*
  - ✓ *Papers that offer at least two moderately elaborated ideas.*
  - ✓ *Papers that present one fully elaborated idea.*

- *These papers have the following characteristics:*

  - ✓ *A reasonably consistent organizational plan.* Occasional inconsistencies may be evident. Responses may also include extraneous or loosely related material.
  - ✓ *Control of written language.* Some errors in spelling, capitalization, punctuation, and/or usage may appear, but they do not unduly distract the reader.
  - ✓ *A clear understanding of the topic, although all parts of the prompt may not be addressed.*

Score Point 2

Responses that are only marginally successful in clarifying, explaining, or providing information about the specified topic.

- *The "2" category is composed of the following kinds of responses:*

  - ✓ *Papers that present a long list of unelaborated ideas, some of which are specific.*
  - ✓ *Papers that present many ideas, most of which are extended.*
  - ✓ *Papers that present just a few ideas, at least one of which is somewhat elaborated.*

Holistic Scale: Four Points *(continued)*

✓ *Papers that only summarize ideas; these papers exhibit no real elaboration.*

■ *The following descriptions characterize a "2" response:*

✓ *A great volume of writing that is not informative in purpose.*

✓ *An organizational plan that does not demonstrate a logical progression of thought; such a response may also exhibit obvious repetition of ideas.* Usually, these inconsistencies do not impede the reader's understanding.

✓ *Marginal control of written language.* Such responses exhibit awkward or simplistic sentence structures and limited word choices. Some errors in spelling, capitalization, punctuation, and/or usage may appear, although these errors do not impede the reader's understanding.

✓ *A limited understanding of the topic or informative task specified in the prompt.*

Score Point 1

Responses that are unsuccessful efforts to clarify, explain, or present information about the specified topic.

■ *The following types of responses fall into the "1" category:*

✓ *Papers in which the writer has employed the wrong mode or misunderstood his or her purpose in writing.* Some of these responses may be persuasive rather than informative. In other responses, the writer does not make any effort to address the specified audience.

✓ *Papers in which the writer attempts to provide expository writing, but does so unsuccessfully.* These responses may appear as any of the following forms:

– *A brief phrase that is related to the prompt.*

– *An overly general response.* Such responses may present one or more ideas, sometimes slightly extended or elaborated, yet they do not address the prompt in any specific or meaningful way. These responses may often appear in the form of a summary or list.

– *A paper that initially focuses on the task but then drifts from the specified topic or from the specified purpose or mode.*

✓ *Papers that lack clarity.* Incomplete or illogical thoughts impede the reader's understanding. In addition, ideas are not connected in explicit or even implicit ways; the reader is confused or completely stymied in comprehending the response.

✓ *Papers in which the writer demonstrates no control of written language.* The reader's comprehension of the paper is seriously impeded by persistent errors in spelling, capitalization, punctuation, and usage.

✓ *Papers that demonstrate no organization or logic.* Such responses may present information in a random or repetitive fashion.

✓ *Papers that show little or no understanding of the topic or informative task specified in the prompt.*

Holistic Scale: Four Points

Score Point 4

Responses that are organized, elaborated, and highly readable attempts to address the persuasive task. Although a "4" paper may exhibit a few inconsistencies, such inconsistencies are eclipsed by the overall quality, coherence, and thoughtfulness of the response.

- *These responses offer a clear position and offer ample and convincing support for that position; all reasons and evidence are relevant and well elaborated. Such responses are also characterized by most of the following:*

  - ✓ *A unified organizational plan.* These responses have a clear organization and seem complete; if the writer employs more than one organizational strategy, all ideas still follow a logical progression. Minor inconsistencies may occur, but they do not detract from the overall order of the paper. Especially well-organized papers that end abruptly may still receive a "4."
  - ✓ *A marked command of written language.* These responses are fluent and clear; although some writers may not use all of the appropriate conventions of language, these responses are nevertheless quite skillfully written.
  - ✓ *Particularly thoughtful or original reasons.* Such reasons may offer an uncommon, philosophical, or wide-ranging perspective on the situation.
  - ✓ *Vivid, relevant details.* All descriptions and arguments are communicated through precise, effective word choices and expressions.
  - ✓ *An unusual persuasive strategy—one that departs from the usual or shows a spark of creative thinking.*
  - ✓ *Attention to all parts of the prompt.*

Score Point 3

Responses that are good efforts in addressing the persuasive task. For the most part, a reader finds the paper clear, coherent, and reasonably elaborated.

- *The "3" category is composed of the following kinds of responses:*

  - ✓ *Papers that offer great number of reasons in support of the writer's position; one may be fully elaborated, several may be somewhat elaborated, or most may be extended.*
  - ✓ *Papers that offer many supporting reasons, most of which are somewhat elaborated.*
  - ✓ *Papers that offer at least two or more moderately elaborated supporting reasons.*
  - ✓ *Responses that present only one fully elaborated reason for the writer's position; this reason must be thoroughly explained and convincing.*

- *These papers have the following characteristics:*

  - ✓ *A reasonably consistent organizational plan.* Occasional inconsistencies may be evident. Responses may also include extraneous or loosely related material.
  - ✓ *Control of written language.* Some errors in spelling, capitalization, punctuation, and/or usage may appear, but they do not unduly distract the reader.
  - ✓ *A clear understanding of the persuasive task, although all parts of the prompt may not be addressed.*

Holistic Scale: Four Points *(continued)*

Score Point 2

Responses that are only marginally successful attempts to address the persuasive task.

- *The following types of responses fall into the "2" category:*
  - ✓ *Papers that present a long list of unelaborated reasons.*
  - ✓ *Papers that present a number of reasons, most of which are extended.*
  - ✓ *Papers that present a few reasons, one of which is somewhat elaborated.*
  - ✓ *Papers that present one moderately elaborated reason.*

- *The following descriptions characterize a "2" response:*
  - ✓ *Writing that is not persuasive in purpose.*
  - ✓ *An organizational plan that does not demonstrate a logical progression of thought; such a response may also exhibit obvious repetition of ideas.* Usually, these inconsistencies do not impede the reader's understanding.
  - ✓ *Marginal control of written language.* Such responses exhibit awkward or simplistic sentence structures and limited word choices. Some errors in spelling, capitalization, punctuation, and/or usage may appear, although these errors do not impede the reader's understanding.
  - ✓ *A limited understanding of the prompt.*

Score Point 1

Responses that are unsuccessful attempts to address the persuasive task.

- *The following types of responses fall into the "1" category:*
  - ✓ *Papers in which the writer has employed the wrong mode or misunderstood his or her purpose in writing.* Some of these responses may expository or narrative rather than persuasive. In other responses, writer gives information that does not support his or her position.
  - ✓ *Papers in which the writer attempts to provide persuasive writing, but does so unsuccessfully.* These responses may appear as any of the following forms:
    - —*A brief phrase that is related to the prompt.*
    - —*An overly general response.* Such responses may present a position and one or more slightly extended reasons, yet the paper does not provide a logical or meaningful case in support of the position. Such responses may often appear as summaries or lists.
    - —*Responses that attend to the task but then drift from the specified topic or from the persuasive purpose.*
  - ✓ *Papers that lack clarity.* Incomplete or illogical thoughts impede the reader's understanding. In addition, ideas are not connected in explicit or even implicit ways; the reader is confused or completely stymied in comprehension.
  - ✓ *Papers in which the writer demonstrates no control of written language.* The reader's comprehension of the paper is seriously impeded by persistent errors in spelling, capitalization, punctuation, and usage.
  - ✓ *Papers that demonstrate no organization or logic.* Such papers may present ideas in a random or repetitive way.
  - ✓ *Papers that show no understanding of the prompt.*

Holistic Scale: Four Points

Score Point 4

A response receiving a score of "4" thoroughly addresses and accurately analyzes all elements required by the prompt. It is focused, organized, perceptive, and well elaborated. Although the paper may exhibit a few inconsistencies, such inconsistencies are eclipsed by the overall quality, coherence, and thoughtfulness of the response.

- *A "4" response is characterized by the following:*

  ✓ *Especially thoughtful or insightful analysis of the elements of the literary work required by the prompt.*

  ✓ *A clear and well-reasoned thesis.*

  ✓ *Clear support for and illustration of the analysis by specific, well elaborated references to the literary work.*

  ✓ *A unified organizational plan.* The responses have a clear organization and seem complete. Minor inconsistencies may occur, but they do not detract from the paper. In cases in which writers have run out of space, especially well-organized papers may still receive a "4."

  ✓ *Stylistic maturity demonstrated by an effective command of sentence structure and diction.* Sentence structure and length are varied; word choice is precise and appropriate to the writer's purpose, occasion, and audience.

  ✓ *A consistent control of the conventions of usage and mechanics in written language.* These responses are fluent and clear; although some writers may not use all of the appropriate conventions of language, these responses are nevertheless quite skillfully written.

Score Point 3

A response receiving a score of "3" addresses all elements required by the prompt and demonstrates a general understanding of the literary work, but the analysis is not as accurate and perceptive as the "4" response. Its focus and organization are less precise as well.

- *Most "3" papers fall into the following categories:*

  ✓ *Papers that offer a great number of points, one of which is moderately elaborated, several of which are somewhat elaborated, or most of which are extended.*

  ✓ *Papers that offer at least two moderately elaborated points.*

  ✓ *Responses that present only one fully elaborated point; this point must be thoroughly explained.*

- *These papers have the following characteristics:*

  ✓ *A logical but not especially insightful analysis of the elements of the literary work required by the prompt.*

  ✓ *A clear thesis.*

  ✓ *A reasonably consistent organizational plan.* Occasional inconsistencies may be evident. Responses may also include extraneous or loosely related material.

  ✓ *Support for and illustration of the main points through specific and accurate references to the literary work.* All such references may not be adequately or effectively elaborated.

  ✓ *A degree of stylistic maturity demonstrated by a basic command of sentence structure and diction.* Word choice is generally precise and sentence structure moderately varied.

  ✓ *A general control of the conventions of written language.* Some errors in grammar, mechanics, and/or usage may appear, but they do not distract the reader.

Holistic Scale: Four Points (continued)

Score Point 2

A response receiving a score of "2" is minimally successful in addressing some elements required by the prompt, but the analysis is often inadequate or inaccurate. The "2" response demonstrates a flawed or incomplete understanding of the literary work.

- *The following types of responses fall into the "2" category:*
  - ✓ *Papers that present a long list of unelaborated ideas.*
  - ✓ *Papers that present many ideas, most of which are extended.*
  - ✓ *Papers that present just a few ideas, at least one of which is somewhat elaborated.*
  - ✓ *Papers that only summarize ideas; these papers exhibit no real elaboration.*

- *Score "2" responses are characterized by any of the following:*
  - ✓ *A minimally successful attempt to analyze one or more of the elements of the literary work as required by the prompt.*
  - ✓ *An imprecise or inaccurate thesis.*
  - ✓ *Supporting evidence from the literary work that is only minimally convincing.* Other supporting evidence may be irrelevant or entirely unconvincing.
  - ✓ *An organizational plan that does not demonstrate a logical progression of thought; such a response may also exhibit obvious repetition of ideas.* Usually, these inconsistencies do not impede the reader's understanding.
  - ✓ *A style characterized by weak or monotonous sentence structure and ineffective diction.* Such responses often contain simple sentences and limited word choices.
  - ✓ *Limited control of the conventions of usage and mechanics in written language as demonstrated by errors in both areas.* Although errors in spelling, capitalization, punctuation, and/or usage may be distracting, these errors do not impede the reader's understanding.

Score Point 1

A response receiving a score of "1" fails to adequately address the elements of the prompt. The response may misrepresent either the prompt or the literary work, or both. It may lack both focus and organization.

- *The "1" response may be characterized by the following:*
  - ✓ *A response in which the writer has misunderstood his or her purpose in writing; the response shows no understanding of literary analysis nor of the interpretive nature of the writing task.*
  - ✓ *A response that has no thesis, asserts a thesis that is not supported by the literary work, or asserts a thesis but fails to support it with evidence from the work.*
  - ✓ *An inaccurate analysis of the literary elements required by the prompt.*
  - ✓ *Inadequate or incomplete support from the literary work.*
  - ✓ *Little or no control over sentence structure, diction, and organization.*
  - ✓ *Poor control over the conventions of mechanics and usage in written language.* The response contains major errors that hinder the reader's comprehension.
  - ✓ *A lack of clarity.* Incomplete or illogical thoughts impede the reader's understanding. In addition, ideas are not connected in explicit or even implicit ways.

Analytical Scale: Six Traits

IDEAS AND CONTENT

Score: 5

The paper is clear, focused, and engaging. Its thoughtful, concrete details capture the reader's attention and flesh out the central theme, main idea, or story line.

- *A score "5" paper has the following characteristics.*

  ✓ The topic is clearly focused and manageable for a paper its kind; it is not overly broad or scattered.
  ✓ Ideas are original and creative.
  ✓ The writer appears to be working from personal knowledge or experience.
  ✓ Key details are insightful and well-considered; they are not obvious, predictable, or humdrum.
  ✓ The development of the topic is thorough and purposeful; the writer anticipates and answers the reader's questions.
  ✓ Supporting details are never superfluous or merely ornamental; every detail contributes to the whole.

Score: 3

The writer develops the topic in a general or basic way; although clear, the paper remains routine or broad.

- *A score "3" paper has the following characteristics.*

  ✓ Although the topic may be fuzzy, it is still possible to understand the writer's purpose and to predict how the paper will be developed.
  ✓ Support is present, but somewhat vague and unhelpful in illustrating the key issues or main idea; the writer makes references to his or her own experience or knowledge, but has difficulty moving from general observations to specifics.
  ✓ Ideas are understandable, yet not detailed, elaborated upon, or personalized; the writer's ideas do not reveal any deep comprehension of the topic or of the writing task.
  ✓ The writer does not stray from the topic, but ideas remain general or slightly implicit; more information is necessary to sketch in the gaps.

Score: 1

The paper does not exhibit any clear purpose or main idea. The reader must use the scattered details to infer a coherent and meaningful message.

- *A score "1" paper has the following characteristics.*

  ✓ The writer seems not to have truly settled on a topic; the essay reads like a series of brainstorming notes or disconnected, random thoughts.
  ✓ The thesis is a vague statement of the topic rather than a main idea about the topic; in addition, there is little or no support or detail.
  ✓ Information is very limited or vague; readers must make inferences to fill in gaps of logic or to identify any progression of ideas.
  ✓ Text may be rambling and repetitious; alternatively, the length may not be adequate for a thoughtful development of ideas.
  ✓ There is no subordination of ideas; every idea seems equally weighted or ideas are not tied to an overarching idea.

Analytical Scale: Six Traits *(continued)*

ORGANIZATION

Score: 5

Organization enables the clear communication of the central idea or story line. The order of information draws the reader effortlessly through the text.

- *A score "5" paper has the following characteristics.*

  ✓ The sequencing is logical and effective; ideas and details "fit " where the writer has placed them.

  ✓ The essay contains an interesting or inviting introduction and a satisfying conclusion.

  ✓ The pacing is carefully controlled; the writer slows down to provide explanation or elaboration when appropriate and increases the pace when necessary.

  ✓ Transitions carefully connect ideas and cue the reader to specific relationships between ideas.

  ✓ The choice of organizational structure is appropriate to the writer's purpose and audience.

  ✓ If present, the title sums up the central idea of the paper in a fresh or thoughtful way.

Score: 3

Organization is reasonably strong; it enables the reader to continually move forward without undue confusion.

- *A score "3" paper has the following characteristics.*

  ✓ The essay has an introduction and conclusion. However, the introduction may not be inviting or engaging; the conclusion may not knit all the paper's ideas together with a summary or restatement.

  ✓ Sequencing is logical, but predictable. Sometimes, the sequence may be so formulaic that it distracts from the content.

  ✓ At times, the sequence may not consistently support the essay's ideas; the reader may wish to mentally reorder sections or to supply transitions as he or she reads.

  ✓ Pacing is reasonably well done, although sometimes the writer moves ahead too quickly or spends too much time on unimportant details.

  ✓ At times, transitions may be fuzzy, showing unclear connections between ideas.

  ✓ If present, the title may be dull or a simple restatement of the topic or prompt.

Score: 1

Writing does not exhibit a sense of purpose or writing strategy. Ideas, details, or events appear to be cobbled together without any internal structure.

- *A score "1" paper has the following characteristics.*

  ✓ Sequencing needs work; one idea or event does not logically follow another. Organizational problems make it difficult for the reader to understand the main idea or story line.

  ✓ There is no real introduction to guide the reader into the paper; neither is there any real conclusion or attempt to tie things up at the end.

  ✓ Pacing is halting or inconsistent; the writer may slow the pace or speed up at inappropriate times.

  ✓ Ideas are connected with confusing transitions; alternatively, connections are altogether absent.

  ✓ If present, the title does not accurately reflect the content.

Analytical Scale: Six Traits *(continued)*

VOICE

Score: 5

The writing is expressive and engaging. In addition, the writer seems to have a clear awareness of audience and purpose.

- **A score "5" paper has the following characteristics.**
  - ✓ The tone of the writing is appropriate for the purpose and audience of the paper.
  - ✓ The reader is aware of a real person behind the text; if appropriate, the writer takes risks in revealing a personal dimension throughout the piece.
  - ✓ If expository or persuasive, the writer shows a strong connection to the topic and explains why the reader should care about the issue.
  - ✓ If narrative writing, the point of view is sincere, interesting, and compelling.

Score: 3

The writer is reasonably genuine, but does not reveal any excitement or connection with the issue. The resulting paper is pleasant, but not truly engaging.

- **A score "3" paper has the following characteristics.**
  - ✓ The writer offers obvious generalities instead of personal insights.
  - ✓ The writer uses neutral language and a slightly flattened tone.
  - ✓ The writer communicates in an earnest and pleasing manner, yet takes no risks. In only rare instances is the reader captivated or moved.
  - ✓ Expository or persuasive writing does not reveal a consistent engagement with the topic; there is no attempt to build credibility with the audience.
  - ✓ Narrative writing doesn't reveal a fresh or individual perspective.

Score: 1

Writing is mechanical or wooden. The writer appears indifferent to the topic and/or the audience.

- **A score "1" paper has the following characteristics.**
  - ✓ The writer shows no concern with the audience; the voice may be jarringly inappropriate for the intended reader.
  - ✓ The development of the topic is so limited that no identifiable point of view is present; or the writing is so short that it offers little but a general introduction of the topic.
  - ✓ The writer seems to speak in a monotone, using a voice that suppresses all excitement about the message.
  - ✓ Although the writing may communicate on a functional level, the writing is ordinary and takes no risks; depending on the topic, it may be overly technical or jargonistic.

Analytical Scale: Six Traits *(continued)*

WORD CHOICE

Score: 5

Words are precise, engaging, and unaffected. They convey the writer's message in an interesting and effective way.

■ *A score "5" paper has the following characteristics.*

✓ All words are specific and appropriate. In all instances, the writer has taken care to choose the right words or phrases.

✓ The paper's language is natural, not overwrought; it never shows a lack of control. Clichés and jargon are rarely used.

✓ The paper contains energetic verbs; precise nouns and modifiers provide clarity.

✓ The writer uses vivid words and phrases, including sensory details; such language creates distinct images in the reader's mind.

Score: 3

Despite its lack of flair, the paper's language gets the message across. It is functional and clear.

■ *A score "3" paper has the following characteristics.*

✓ Words are correct and generally adequate, but lack originality or precision.

✓ Familiar words and phrases do not pique the reader's interest or imagination. Lively verbs and phrases perk things up occasionally, but the paper does not consistently sparkle.

✓ There are attempts at engaging or academic language but they sometimes seem overly showy or pretentious.

✓ The writing contains passive verbs, basic nouns and adjectives, and the lack of precise adverbs.

Score: 1

The writer's limited vocabulary impedes communication; he or she seems to struggle for words to convey a clear message.

■ *A score "1" paper has the following characteristics.*

✓ Vague language communicates an imprecise or incomplete message. The reader is left confused or unsure of the writer's purpose.

✓ Words are used incorrectly. In addition, frequent misuse of parts of speech impair understanding.

✓ Excessive redundancy in the paper is distracting.

✓ The writing overuses jargon or clichés.

Analytical Scale: Six Traits (continued)

SENTENCE FLUENCY

- *A score "5" paper has the following characteristics.*

Score: 5

Sentences are thoughtfully constructed and sentence structure is varied throughout the paper. When read aloud, the writing is fluent and rhythmic.

✓ The sentences are constructed so that meaning is clear to the reader.

✓ Sentences vary in length and in structure.

✓ Varied sentence beginnings add interest and clarity.

✓ The writing has a steady beat; the reader is able to read the text effortlessly, without confusion or stumbling.

✓ Dialogue, if used, is natural. Any fragments are used purposefully and contribute to the paper's style.

✓ Thoughtful connectives and transitions between sentences reveal how the paper's ideas work together.

- *A score "3" paper has the following characteristics.*

Score: 3

The text maintains a steady rhythm, but the reader may find it more flat or mechanical than fluent or musical.

✓ Sentences are usually grammatical and unified, but they are routine rather than artful. The writer has not paid a great deal of attention to how the sentences sound.

✓ There is some variation in sentence length and structure as well as in sentence beginnings. Not all sentences are constructed exactly the same way.

✓ The reader may have to search for transitional words and phrases that show how sentences relate to one another. Sometimes, such context clues are entirely absent when they should be present.

✓ Although sections of the paper invite expressive oral reading, the reader may also encounter many wooden or awkward sections.

- *A score "1" paper has the following characteristics.*

Score: 1

The reader will encounter challenges in reading the choppy or confusing text; meaning may be significantly obscured by the errors in sentence construction.

✓ The sentences do not "hang together." They are run-on, incomplete, monotonous, or awkward.

✓ Phrasing often sounds too sing-song, not natural. The paper does not invite expressive oral reading.

✓ Nearly all the sentences begin the same way and they may all follow the same pattern (e.g. subject-verb-object). The result may be a monotonous repetition of sounds.

✓ Endless connectives or a complete lack of connectives create a confused muddle of language.

Analytical Scale: Six Traits *(continued)*

CONVENTIONS

Score: 5

Standard writing conventions (e.g. spelling, punctuation, capitalization, grammar, usage, and paragraphing) are used correctly and in a way that aids the reader's understanding. Any errors tend to be minor; the piece is nearly ready for publication.

■ *A score "5" paper has the following characteristics.*

✓ Paragraphing is regular and enhances the organization of the paper.

✓ Grammar and usage are correct and add clarity to the text as a whole. Sometimes, the writer may manipulate conventions in a controlled way—especially grammar and spelling—for stylistic effect.

✓ Punctuation is accurate; it enables the reader to move through the text with understanding and ease.

✓ The writer's understanding of capitalization skills is evident throughout the paper.

✓ Most words, even difficult ones, are spelled correctly.

✓ The writing is long and complex enough to show the writer using a wide range of conventions skillfully.

Score: 3

The writer exhibits an awareness of a limited set of standard writing conventions and uses them to enhance the paper's readability. Although the writer shows control, at times errors distract the reader or impede communication. Moderate editing is required for publication.

■ *A score "3" paper has the following characteristics.*

✓ Paragraphs are used, but may begin in the wrong places or run together sections that should be separate paragraphs.

✓ Conventions may not be correct all of the time. However, problems with grammar and usage are usually not serious enough to distort meaning.

✓ Terminal (end-of-sentence) punctuation is usually correct; internal punctuation (e.g. commas, apostrophes, semicolons, parentheses) may be missing or wrong.

✓ On common words, spelling is usually correct or phonetic.

✓ Most words are capitalized correctly, but the writer's command of more sophisticated capitalization skills is inconsistent.

Score 1

There are errors in spelling, punctuation, usage and grammar, capitalization, and/or paragraphing that seriously impede the reader's comprehension. Extensive editing is required for publication.

■ *A score "1" paper has the following characteristics.*

✓ Paragraphing is missing, uneven, or too frequent. Most of the paragraphs do not reinforce or support the organizational structure of the paper.

✓ Errors in grammar/usage are very common and distracting; such errors also affect the paper's meaning.

✓ Punctuation, including terminal punctuation, is often missing or incorrect.

✓ Even on common words, spelling errors are frequent.

✓ Capitalization is haphazard or reveals the writer's understanding of only the simplest rules.

✓ The paper must be read once just to decode the language and then again to capture the paper's meaning.

Notes on Writing Assessment Scales

Use this and the following page to extend and adjust the criteria for writing provided in the scales on pages 145–162. Or just jot some notes about criteria you want to pay special attention to as you read the essays ahead.

_____

_____

_____

_____

_____

_____

_____

_____

_____

_____

_____

_____

_____

_____

_____

_____

_____

_____

_____

_____

_____

_____

_____

_____

_____

_____

_____

_____

_____

_____

_____

Notes on Writing Assessment Scales (continued)

Sample A: Expository Writing

Having your driver's license or learner's permit has many benefits, but it also entails many responsibilities. Write a well-organized composition explaining both the benefits and the responsibilities of driving.

The Responsibilities and Benefits of a Driver's License

When you first walk outside from the Department of Public Safety, you stand looking at what you hold in your hand—your first driver's license. When you look up, you see your future stretching before you: Freedom! Independence! Respect! Something else is also lying ahead: Responsibility. Getting behind the wheel of an automobile certainly comes with many benefits, but it requires a great deal of responsibility also. Not only do you have to train for getting your license, you must realize that you hold the lives of others and yourself in your hands and that other people are trusting you to drive safely. In return, you have the freedom to run errands as you need, you have independence from relying on your parents or friends for rides, and you have people, especially younger brothers and sisters, regarding you with admiration and respect. But first comes the responsiblity.

Getting a driver's license requires a great deal of a teenager's time and effort. Multitudes of first drivers take the classes and behind-the-wheel training required for the license. Completing the requirements can take from six weeks to four months. First, you sit in a classroom listening to lectures, reading the driver's ed manual, and watching videos that show you proper driving techniques and an accident's blood and gore. Then you spend long hours in a tiny car with an oversized driving instructor and three other teenagers, all giggling at your embarrassing mistakes. Over and over you hear, "You are toying with a large machine. Don't drive recklessly because you have your life, as well as the lives of others, in your hands." If that sense of responsibility isn't enough, your family begins to repeat, "Drive carefully. You cannot toy with people's lives for a few moments of being cool." You wait for the day when your family finally says, "We trust you."

Sample A: Expository Writing *(continued)*

Despite the grueling work to learn responsibilities of having a driver's license, the benefits are worth it. At last, you can go places on the spur of the moment. If you need to run to the store to pick up a book you need for English class, you can just hop in your car and go. Freedom! You no longer have to work your schedule around the schedule of your family. You can even give rides to your friends to school and sports activities. Independence! And best of all for your family, you can chauffeur your younger siblings to dance lessons, friends' houses, and to school. When they arrive at school, their friends are really impressed and look at you with . . . respect! Best of all for you, when drivers in your neighborhood see your wonderful and miraculous driving, they will not mutter under their breath "Teenagers, BAH!" but will be proud of you as a responsible driver. Now, that's a benefit.

Sample A Evaluation: Expository Writing

Six Point Holistic Scale

Rating: 6 points

Comments: The writer focuses on the topic in an engaging and controlled way, thoroughly elaborating on the many benefits and responsibilities of having a driver's license. Each point is fully and cleverly illustrated with examples and anecdotes from the writer's personal experience. The paper's organization is logical, and the sentences are varied and smoothly constructed. The tone is informal and fresh throughout, and it shows a sly awareness of audience. The writer is clearly in command of the conventions of written language.

Four Point Holistic Scale

Rating: 4 points

Comments: The writer uses specific, relevant examples to elaborate the many benefits and responsibilities of having a driver's license. Both responsiblities and benefits are elaborated with vivid, concrete, and cleverly-expressed examples drawn from a teenager's personal experience. The paper's organization is logical; sentence structure is varied and incorporates quotations to good effect. The writer demonstrates control over various conventions of written language, using fragments and dashes in an appropriate and sophisticated way.

Six Trait Analytic Scale

Ratings

Ideas and Content: 5	**Word Choice: 5**
Organization: 5	**Sentence Fluency: 5**
Voice: 5	**Conventions: 5**

Comments: The writer's approach to the task of explaining the benefits and responsibilities of having a driver's license is fresh and original, obviously based on the writer's experience. The organization demonstrates a clear and logical progression of thought. The writer also uses clever opening and closing paragraphs and provides clear and elegant transitions between the paragraphs. The voice is obviously an entertaining and personal one, but appropriate for the informal tone adopted in the paper. The language is lively and precise. The sentences are fluent; complex sentences are frequently balanced by short well-placed ones. The writer also follows the conventions of spelling, grammar, and punctuation, and shows control in the use of ellipses and dashes for dramatic effect.

Sample B: Expository Writing

PROMPT

Having your driver's license or learner's permit has many benefits, but it also entails many responsibilities. Write a well-organized composition explaining both the benefits and the responsibilities of driving.

Getting a Driver's License

Getting behind the wheel of an automobile requires a great deal of responsibility, but it comes with many benefits. Responsibility is the key to having and keeping a driver's license and/or learner's permit. The responsibilities include taking time and effort to get a license, realizing that the lives of others and yourself are being put into your hands, and finally having people trust in you to drive safely. With that responsibility comes many benefits. The benefits are being able to drive to a place without relying on your parents or friends, being able to go places you wish with your friends, and having people look at you with admiration.

The responsibility of obtaining and keeping a driver's license is a titanic event in a young person's life. In the first place, the teenager spends having a great deal of time and effort to get a license. The effort is not in the long hours of being spent in a tiny car with a driving instructor and three other teenagers, but in the learning the material, watching driving videos, and gaining countless hours of observation and driving skills. Another key in responsibility, which is probably the biggest, is that you are toying with a large machine and are putting your life in danger, as well as the lives of others, by driving recklessly. If a wreck should happen, the amount of guilt and burden that will be put onto your shoulders will be very overbearing. Lastly, people in your family and on the road put their trust into your responsible driving. You cannot toy with people's lives for a few moments of being cool.

Although, having a license requires much responsibility, receiving the benefits are worth the responsibilities. To help better illustrate the benefits, consider the wonders of receiving a driver's license. In the first place, you can drive to places without relying on

Sample B: Expository Writing *(continued)*

your parents or friends. This will benefit you, your friends, and your parents. You will have the satisfaction of helping your parents. You can also help your friends by giving them lifts to school and other places. You will help your parents by giving your younger siblings a ride to school. Second, you can go places whenever you want to. Lastly, people on the road will look at you with a higher regard and admiration. They will see your wonderful and miraculous driving and see that you are a responsible and carefree driver.

To conclude, having a driver's license takes a tremendous amount of responsibility and yet the treasures are spectacular. It takes time, effort, and trust by your friends and family to prove the responsibility portion of driving. The benefits will come with time.

Sample B Evaluation: Expository Writing

Six Point Holistic Scale

Rating: 4 points

Comments: The writing focuses on the topic and thoughtfully discusses the responsibilities and benefits of having a driver's license. The writer presents a number of specific ideas, most of which are moderately elaborated. Although the support is somewhat general in nature, the writer is clearly engaged with the topic and aware of his audience. The word choices reflect a teenager's intense feelings about this experience but are some-what exaggerated, such as "very overbearing." In general, the writer adheres to the conventions of written language.

Four Point Holistic Scale

Rating: 4 points

Comments: The writer presents a set of moderately elaborated explanations of the benefits and responsibilities of having a driver's license. The paper's organization is logical and con-tains adequate opening and closing paragraphs. The writer shows control over the language, despite several exaggerated word choices, such as the "wonderful and miraculous driv-ing." With a few exceptions, the writer uses acceptable punctu-ation, grammar, and spelling.

Six Trait Analytic Scale

Ratings

Ideas and Content: 4	**Word Choice: 3**
Organization: 4	**Sentence Fluency: 4**
Voice: 3	**Conventions: 4**

Comments: The writer has clearly focused on the benefits and responsibilities of having a driver's license, although most of the observations are general in nature and sometimes the read-er wants more precise examples. The introduction and conclu-sion are clearly recognizable, although a bit repetitive. The sequence of ideas is also clear. The writer communicates in an earnest and pleasing manner, revealing the emotion that such a topic prompts in teenagers. The familiar phrases and colorful word choices, such as "titanic," "spectacular," and "treasures," are sometimes exaggerated and show a lack of control. The sentences are grammatical, showing some variety in length and complexity. The paragraphing is obvious, and the writer usually follows the conventions of usage, spelling, and mechanics.

Sample C: Expository Writing

PROMPT

Having your driver's license or learner's permit has many benefits, but it also entails many responsibilities. Write a well-organized composition explaining both the benefits and the responsibilities of driving.

One time I got my learner's permit. Then it took a long time to get my drivers' lisence. What took so long? Responsibel. Responsibel is the key to getting and keeping a drivers licence an/or learner's permit. The responsibels include 1) taking time and effort, 2) the lives of others and yourself are being put into you're hands. The benefits are 1) you can drive to a place without relying on you're parents or friends, 2) you will also be able to go places your self. This being so, here are the further examples of having a driver's license.

In the first place, a drive'rs license takes a lot of time and effort. The great deal of time it takes to get your licence is overwhelming. It took me six months to get my lisense. Because the school wrecked the cars and the teachers quit. It was a mess, and I coulnd't get no help." The effort is the learning of the material. Yet, another key in responsibelty, which is probably the biggest, is that you toying with a large machine and putting you're life, as well as the lives of others, by driving recklessly. If your in a wreck, you take the responsibel of putting the lives of the victims into you're hands! The amount of guilt and burden that will be put onto you're shoulders will be very over-bearing!

Here are examples to portray the wonders of receiving a driver's license. 1) You can drive to places without relying on you're parents or friends. 2) You can go places by yourself. They will see you're wonderful and miraculous driving and see that you are a responsibel.

To conclude, having a driver's license takes a lot of responsibel. The benefits too. I hope this paper will show you what it takes to own a drivers' lisence.

Sample C Evaluation: Expository Writing

Six Point Holistic Scale

Rating: 2 points

Comments: The writer understands the topic and attempts to provide examples of both the responsibilities and the benefits of having a driver's license. The writer elaborates briefly upon one benefit, but then drifts off-topic in the second paragraph. The writer attempts to impose an organization by numbering ideas, but the ideas are skeletal and redundant. At times, the writer's ideas also lack clarity. Diction is imprecise and there are frequent and blatant errors in grammar, usage, punctuation, and spelling.

Four Point Holistic Scale

Rating: 2 points

Comments: The writer addresses the responsibilities and benefits of having a driver's license, but seems to stray from a true expository course, lapsing into narrative. The writing sometimes lacks clarity and occasionally jumps from one idea to another, depite the numbering system the writer uses to organize the sequence of ideas. Support is minimal and vague. The writer also lacks control over diction, sentence structure, punctuation, grammar, usage, and spelling.

Six Trait Analytic Scale

Ratings

Ideas and Content: 1	**Word Choice: 1**
Organization: 1	**Sentence Fluency: 1**
Voice: 1	**Conventions: 1**

Comments: The writer attempts to explain the responsibilities and benefits of having a driver's license, but the writing is at times disconnected and unclear. In some paragraphs, the sequencing of ideas drifts away from the expository purpose. The lead and conclusion show a faint awareness of audience, but are too redundant or brief to be effective. The writer's voice communicates only on a functional level and struggles to use a consistent tone. The word choices are fairly simple, and the sentence structure includes awkward phrasing and ineffective fragments. The writer makes serious errors in spelling, punctuation, grammar, and usage.

Notes on Expository Writing

Use this page to jot notes about the expository essays and evaluations you have just read. How would you evaluate them?

_____

_____

_____

_____

_____

_____

_____

_____

_____

_____

_____

_____

_____

_____

_____

_____

_____

_____

_____

_____

_____

_____

_____

_____

_____

_____

_____

_____

_____

_____

Sample A: Persuasive Writing

PROMPT

Should the United States spend money on space exploration? Some people think the new discoveries and technologies gained from space exploration are worth the expense. Others believe that the money should be spent to relieve poverty. Write a well-organized essay in which you state and give reasons for your position on this issue.

Space Exploration or Poverty Relief?

As a citizen of the United States, I am concerned about our government's issues that affect our country's and people's future. Our government's latest debate is very important: should the government spend its money on space exploration or on relieving poverty? Basing my response to this question on our heritage in the U.S., our common sense, and our humanitan spirit, I believe that the government should not waste useful money on futile attempts at space exploration, but spend its money more wisely on solving the problem of world poverty.

Millions of people in the world are leading lives in poverty by no fault of theirs, but because they have never been given a chance to rise out of their station in life. The United States was founded upon the principles of self-rights and equal opportunity for people. Are we just going to let those ideals apply only to Americans or are we able to use that same spirit our forefathers instilled in us to aid millions of people worldwide? According to a recent statistic in a 1999 issue of Time, 65% of the people who live in poverty are not being helped. This statistic is alarmingly high, and unfortunately, the truth. If these human beings are not helped, then what hope do they have of ever having a life without the pressures and restraints that poverty inflicts?

In addition, space exploration takes up too much time and too much money from our country's resources. Even with today's technology, it takes years for a space mission to go to the outskirts of our known universe. In those precious years, many of the world's needy could be saved by redirecting the funds now spent on space exploration. For example, NASA has recently suffered the loss of the Mars Polar Lander,

Sample A: Persuasive Writing *(continued)*

at the cost of billions of dollars, in a futile space exploration mission. Out in space, many variables stand in the path of these explorers. For example, the satellite's machinery might malfunction, as in the case of the Polar Lander, or the satellite itself might drift off course. According to a 2000 issue of <u>Space and Science</u>, the government is spending several billions of dollars annually in space exploration. Common sense indicates that a sum like that could easily take away the problem of poverty worldwide. Space exploration is never a guarantee, so I believe that we should take care of our own planet's problems before we take a step into another universe, looking for new problems to fix.

Finally, I feel that our money should be redirected to the care of poverty-stricken people because it's the humanitarian thing to do. Imagine this example: A computer sitting next to a starving child who is so weak that he cannot even cry out for food. Which one is worth more? In the human heart, does that expensive computer really outweigh the few pennies given to help that hungry child? If so, then how can we uphold our sense of justice, only to ignore it when needy people do not fit our agenda? Our government needs to forget the policies and the debates that show our hesitancy to perform humanitarian acts. What these people need is action. Immediately. Besides, clever as he is, HAL (from <u>2001: A Space Odyssey</u>) does not have feelings to hurt if we neglect him.

Beyond the mysteries of the sun, moon, planets, and stars, there is suffering back at home, all around Earth. Never has the poverty problem been solved. Now is the time to redeem that failure. We have the chance to take something bad and to make something good. It is not a decision to be reached by calculations and a click of a button, but of human values and the human heart. Mars can wait; these people cannot.

Sample A Evaluation: Persuasive Writing

Six Point Holistic Scale

Rating: 6 points

Comments: The writing is focused, purposeful, and persuasive. The essay addresses the prompt with a philosophical thoughtfulness and control; the writer takes a clear position and adheres to this position throughout, even pointing out flaws in the opposing argument for funding space exploration. The paper's organizational pattern demonstrates a logical progression of ideas, and the support consists of statistics from reliable secondary sources, concrete illustrations, and relevant examples. The writer shows a strong commitment to the subject by offering a series of emotional and ethical appeals and by concluding with a call to action. The paper's style reveals a mature command of language. The sentence structure is varied, and fragments are used purposefully for dramatic effect. Few, if any, convention errors occur in mechanics, usage, and punctuation.

Four Point Holistic Scale

Rating: 4 points

Comments: The writer has addressed the persuasive task in a unified and highly readable way. The response provides a clear position and convincing support in the form of thoughtful, specific reasons and well-elaborated, relevant examples. The writer also makes illuminating and evocative emotional and ethical appeals, such as the comparison of the computer and starving child's worth. The paper is logically organized and shows a consistent control of written language.

Six Trait Analytic Scale

Ratings

Ideas and Content: 5	**Word Choice: 5**
Organization: 4	**Sentence Fluency: 5**
Voice: 5	**Conventions: 5**

Comments: The essay is clear and focused, and it contains many insightful and well-considered details. The organization is logically sequenced, linking the three body paragraphs to key reasons in the thesis statement—the American tenet of opportunity for all, common sense, and a humanitarian spirit. The writer's tone is expressive, engaging, and shows an awareness of audience. The writer's language is precise, interesting, and natural. The sentence structure is varied and musical, especially in the writer's deliberate use of fragments and short, emphatic sentences. The writer effectively uses the conventions of spelling, punctuation, grammar, usage, and paragraphing to enhance readability.

Sample B: Persuasive Writing

PROMPT

Should the United States spend money on space exploration? Some people think the new discoveries and technologies gained from space exploration are worth the expense. Others believe that the money should be spent to relieve poverty. Write a well-organized essay in which you state and give reasons for your position on this issue.

The Cost of Space Exploration

As a citizen of the United States, I am concerned in our government's issues. It is issues like these which affect our country's and people's future. I agree how every side should be heard out, but, I am writing to convey my own opinion. How should the government spend its money, on space exploration or on relieving poverty? I personally think the government should not waste money on space exploration, but on dissolving the problem of world poverty.

The first reason I think that is because millions of people in the world are leading lives in horrible poverty by no fault of theirs, but because they have never been given a chance to rise out of their station in life. One of the main foundations of our government is self-rights and equal opportunity for people. Are we just going to let those ideals apply only to Americans or are we able to use that same spirit of our forefathers to aid millions of people worldwide? On tv every day we see stories of disasters and hungry people. If these human beings are not helped, then what hope do they have of ever having a life without the pressures and restraints that poverty brings?

I also believe space exploration takes up too much time and too much money. Even with today's technology, it takes years for a satellite to go to the outside edges of our known universe or even to a close planet. In those precious years, many of the world's poor and needy could be saved. Also with space exploration, there is no absolute certain guarantee of successful results. For example, the satellite's machine might disfunction,

Sample B: Persuasive Writing *(continued)*

or the satellite itself might drift off course. Then all that money was spent, but for nothing. And nothing comes of nothing. Besides, since when have you ever heard of how the technology gained from space exploration helped feed anybody in Africa or India, or even in America? Space exploration is never a bonified guarantee, so I believe that we should take care of our own planet's problems before we try to visit into another universe.

Finally, I feel that our money should be used to the care of poverty-stricken people because it's the human thing to do. Is a computer that important to sacrifice a starving nation for? Compare a computer sitting next to a starving child who is so weak that he cannot even cry out for food and decide which thing is worth more? Does that expensive computer really outweigh help for that hungry child? If so, then how can we agree to a sense of justice, only to ignore it when people in need do not fit our agenda? Our government needs to forget the policies that slow our need to perform human acts.

To sum up, beyond the mysteries of space, there is suffering back at home, all around Earth. Even though you hear that the poor are with you always, never has the poverty problem been solved. Now is the time to fix the problem. We have the chance to take something bad and to make something good. Hopefully, we can make a difference and help a hungry child.

Sample B Evaluation: Persuasive Writing

Six Point Holistic Scale

Rating: 4 points

Comments: The writing is generally focused on the persuasive task, and the paper exhibits some sense of completeness. The essay demonstrates a coherent organizational pattern, but the support for each point is general and the elaboration is erratic. The word choices are adequate, though sometimes vague and plagued with a few diction problems, such as "dissolving the problem." The sentence patterns demonstrate no real stylistic sophistication. Some errors in punctuation, spelling, and grammar consistently occur, but the writer has a general grasp of the conventions of written language.

Four Point Holistic Scale

Rating: 3 points

Comments: The essay addresses the persuasive task in a thoughtful way, and the reader has no difficulty in understanding the writer's position. The writer presents several reasons, but the elaborations are somewhat vague, without the benefit of precise detail. The essay's organization is logical and the writer is careful to use recognizable transitions between paragraphs. Although the writer's voice clearly shows an understanding of the persuasive task, the essay does exhibit some distracting errors in punctuation, spelling, and grammar.

Six Trait Analytic Scale

Ratings

Ideas and Content: 3	**Word Choice: 3**
Organization: 3	**Sentence Fluency: 3**
Voice: 4	**Conventions: 3**

Comments: The writer addresses the topic in a thoughtful way and offers a clear opinion. However, the writer's ideas are based on general observations, with few specifics to illustrate the main ideas. The introduction and conclusion are brief, but recognizable; the essay uses obvious transitions between most paragraphs. The writer's voice is sincere, with some measure of concern about the topic, but he relies on generalities instead of personal insights. The essay's language is functional, with some lapses in diction or phrasing. The sentences are usually grammatical and routine, with some sentence variety. The writer has some difficulty with the conventions of spelling and punctuation. Other conventions of grammar and usage are generally correct, although minor errors are evident.

Sample C: Persuasive Writing

PROMPT

Should the United States spend money on space exploration? Some people think the new discoveries and technologies gained from space exploration are worth the expense. Others believe that the money should be spent to relieve poverty. Write a well-organized essay in which you state and give reasons for your position on this issue.

Space Travel

Should the government spend its money on space exploration or to releive poverty? Some people think the new discoveries and technlogies gained from space exploriation are worth the expence. I am going to state what I beleive and give my reasons on this issue.

Poverty is a terrible life force. Millions of people in the world are leding lives in horrible poverty by no fault of them, but because they can't try to rise out of their station in life. The Americans who fought for this country had ideals. One idea is self-rights. Self-rights apply to Americans just as they did to our four fathers. Are we just going to let those ideals apply only to Americans or are we able to use them to help millions of people worldwide? On "TV" every day we see stories of disasters and hungry people. Yesterday I saw a whole program on starvation in Africa. It was terrible. We should help these people. We should send money to them, and pay them to get food. Then, no starvation for them to be in.

Space exploration is a very big deal in our country, which costs a lot of money. We should spend that money on the world's poor and needy so they could be saved. Have you ever tasted space food like astronauts eat? It is weird. We could save the space food and send it to the hungry people. That would save a lot of money on the wierd tasteing food. Also with space travel is dangerous. No absolute certain guarantee of returning. For example, the space ship might crash, or blow up, or drift off course!!! Then all that money was spent for nothing. And no-thing comes of nothing. In America? So I believe that we should take care of problems here on earth before we

Sample C: Persuasive Writing *(continued)*

try to visit a completely diffrent solar system.

 Finally my reason is because our money should be used to the care of poverty people because it's the right thing to do to them. What's it worth to you? Does that expensive computer really weigh more in your minds than the money that help that hungry child? If not, then we need to be human and quit argueing about space and poverty.

 To sum up, we need to fix the poor people and their problem by not going into space any more. That is why it is not worth the expence, even if there are new discoveries. I hope you agree with me about poverty.

Sample C Evaluation: Persuasive Writing

Six Point Holistic Scale

Rating: 2 points

Comments: The essay attempts to come to terms with the persuasive task and the topic, but the writing is ill-focused and jumpy. The paper also contains a significant digression in its discussion of "space food." Little, if any organizational pattern exists. The essay also suffers from limited word choices and blatant errors in sentence structure, grammar, and usage. Commonly used words are misspelled.

Four Point Holistic Scale

Rating: 2 points

Comments: The essay attempts to address the persuasive task, but the paper lacks focus and control. The topic is addressed in an incoherent or random fashion, with ideas and support often only loosely tied to the writer's position or persuasive task. Although the essay uses signal words, such as "Finally" and "To sum up," the organization does not provide a logical progression of ideas or clear transition. The essay also demonstrates a limited control of the conventions of sentence structure, grammar, usage, spelling, and mechanics.

Six Trait Analytic Scale

Ratings

Ideas and Content: 1	**Word Choice: 1**
Organization: 1	**Sentence Fluency: 1**
Voice: 2	**Conventions: 2**

Comments: The essay has no clear sense of purpose and appears to be a series of very loosely connected thoughts or brainstorming ideas. The main idea restates the prompt with vague and confusing supporting details. The paper's organization consists of a series of ideas loosely strung together, without a fully realized introduction or conclusion. The voice hints at an enthusiasm for the writer's persuasive stance; overall, however, the writing only communicates on a functional level. The word choices are imprecise or incorrect. The sentence structure is choppy, rambling, and awkward. The essay violates the conventions of spelling, punctuation, grammar, and usage. Extensive editing would be required for publication.

Notes on Persuasive Writing

Use this page to jot notes about the persuasive essays and evaluations you have just read. How would you evaluate the essays?

_____

_____

_____

_____

_____

_____

_____

_____

_____

_____

_____

_____

_____

_____

_____

_____

_____

_____

_____

_____

_____

_____

_____

_____

_____

_____

_____

_____

_____

_____

_____

_____

_____

_____

Sample A: Literary Analysis

PROMPT

One way that writers reveal character is through the characters' actions. From the novels, short stories, plays, poems, and biographies you have read, select a work in which character is revealed by action. Describe the character and use specific references from the work to show how the character's actions reveal his or her nature. The work you choose must be from world literature other than British (England, Ireland, Scotland, Wales) literature and American (United States) literature.

The Consequences of Character: Creon in Sophocles' Antigone

The tragedies of the Greek playwright Sophocles both entertained and educated his audiences. One of his most famous plays, Antigone, educated the audience about the character of a king by showing them traits of character a leader should not have. Creon, the newly crowned king of Thebes, shows by his actions that arrogance, paranoia, and stubbornness are not the traits of a successful ruler.

The play opens the day after the great battle between Polyneices and his brother Eteocles for the throne of Thebes. Circumstances have made Creon, their uncle, king. Although Creon might at first appear to be a strong and decisive leader, his initial act as king actually shows his arrogance. He decrees that Eteocles, who defended the City, will be buried with full military honors, but Polyneices, who attacked the city, is to be left to rot, unburied, an action against the religious laws of the day. Creon arrogantly believes that he can judge the dead by denying them the rites demanded by the gods. Later, he tells Teiresias that "if the great eagles of God himself / Should carry him [Polyneices] stinking bit by bit to heaven," he would not change his decree.

Creon's actions also reveal another dangerous trait in a king—a paranoid personality. Even as he tells the Chorus of his decree, he expects someone to break it. He demands that the Chorus give no support to whoever breaks this law. His paranoia leads him to believe that "money talks, and the wisest" can be bribed. Further evidence of his paranoia is revealed when he accuses the guard who reports the burial and Teiresias who warns him that the gods are offended by the unburied bodies of having

Sample A: Literary Analysis *(continued)*

taken bribes. He has no logical reason or evidence to support either accusation.

Creon reveals his final weakness, stubbornness, most obviously through his interaction with his son Haimon. Haimon, Antigone's fiancee, comes to reason with his father, he argues from the point of view of what is good for his father. Haimon tells his father that throughout the city people are questioning the king's treatment of Antigone. They believe that instead of death she should have "all the honor that we can give her." Haimon begs his father to listen to reason. Even the Choragos advises Creon to listen to Haimon, but Creon stubbornly refuses, asking sarcastically if he should "go to school to a boy" or allow the City to "teach me how to rule," when his "voice is the one voice giving orders in this City!"

Even when Teiresias warns Creon that he will pay "with flesh of [his] own flesh," Creon stubbornly persists in arrogant confidence. When the Choragos says he cannot remember that Teiresias was ever "false," Creon becomes fearful and asks for advice. The Choragos advices him to first free Antigone and then bury Polyneices. Arrogant and stubborn to the end, Creon buries the body first. By the time he gets to Antigone, he is too late. He pays a heavy price for his flaws: the suicides of his son and his wife.

Sample A Evaluation: Literary Analysis

Six Point Holistic Scale

Rating: 6 points

Comments: The essay addresses the prompt by thoughtfully analyzing a character from a work of world literature—Sophocles's *Antigone*—through the character's actions. The paper is focused and shows a great deal of insight into the literary work. The thesis is clear and shows an awareness of how characterization is revealed in a literary work. Each paragraph in the body supports the thesis by naming a character trait and explaining how it is revealed by Creon's actions. Each paragraph also presents well-elaborated evidence from the text of the play. The quotations chosen for support are particularly apt and well integrated into the paper. The style of the essay is quite mature. Organization is logical and sentence structure and diction are varied and effective.

Four Point Holistic Scale

Rating: 4 points

Comments: The essay perceptively addresses and analyzes a character from world literature through his actions, as required by the prompt. The thesis is clear and effectively supported by specific references—often in the form of well-chosen quotations—to the literary work. These references are also thoroughly elaborated, showing the writer's insight into the work. Organization is clear and logical throughout the essay. The style of the essay is mature in its command of sentence structures and diction. The few flaws in the essay are minor errors in usage or mechanics.

Six Trait Analytic Scale

Ratings

Ideas and Content: 5	**Word Choice: 5**
Organization: 5	**Sentence Fluency: 5**
Voice: 5	**Conventions: 5**

Comments: The paper focuses exclusively on the character of Creon and supports its main ideas with well-selected details from the text of the play. The paper's organization is logical and effective, giving the reader a sense of completeness at the end. The tone of the analysis is appropriately objective and direct. The writer is clearly knowledgeable about his topic and in control of his argument. The writer's diction is appropriate for his purpose; all word choices are precise and engaging. The structure of the sentences is varied and all sentences read smoothly and flow one into the other naturally. The writer clearly knows and observes the conventions of writing.

Sample B: Literary Analysis

Creon's Consequences

The Greek playwright Sophocles wrote many plays. One of his most famous plays, <u>Antigone</u>, shows his ideas about the characteristics of a leader, King Creon. Sophocles shows us through King Creon's actions that Creon does not have the character to be a good leader.

The play opens the day after Polyneices and his army attacks the city of Thebes. His brother, Eteocles, defends the city. Polyneices and Eteocles kill each other in the battle and Polyneices's army is defeated. Creon becomes the new king. At first Creon appears to be a strong leader, but he is really arrogant. Creon orders that Etocles will be buried with full military honors, but Polyneices will be left on the ground to rot. This action was against their religious laws. Creon looks like a strong leader. However, he wants the people to support his treatment of Polyneices' body even though he did not ask them first.

Creon's actions also show that he is paranoid. For example, he accuses the guard who reports the buriel of Polyneices's body of taking a bribe to bury the body, but he has no evidence. He also thinks Antigone's sister Ismene is as guilty as Antigone, but without evidence. When the profit Teiresias advise Creon to think about changing his mind, Creon accuses him of taking a bribe to say that. Teiresias tells him about the meat not burning at the alter, too.

Creon is also stubborn and it shows when he talks to Antigone or his son Haimon. He is so stubborn he will not listen to Antigone's reasons for buring Polyneices. He will

Sample B: Literary Analysis *(continued)*

not even think he might be wrong. Instead, he says she is being pridful and that she must die. Haimon comes to talk to his father. Creon tells his son that law and order must come before anything, even family. Then Haimon tells his father that the whole city is on Antigone's side, but Creon won't budge. He thinks Haimon is stupid for selling out to a woman.

Creon's words and actions shows what kind of man he really is. He is arrogant, paranoid, and stubborn. Not to mention stupid. He looses his family because when Antigone kills herself, Haimon does, too. Also Creon's wife kills herself when she hears about her son. She curses Creon before she dies which makes him wish he was dead.

Sample B Evaluation: Literary Analysis

Six Point Holistic Scale

Rating: 4 points

Comments: The essay addresses the prompt by analyzing a character from a work of world literature through the character's actions. The essay is generally focused and has a thesis which each paragraph in the body attempts to support. The thesis, however, is somewhat vague and all support is minimally elaborated. The writing adequately communicates the writer's thoughts, but the style is unsophisticated. In particular, sentence structure and diction are monotonous. The essay generally follows the conventions of usage and mechanics although there are breakdowns, including some misspelled words, a fragment, errors in agreement, and a comma splice.

Four Point Holistic Scale

Rating: 3 points

Comments: The essay addresses and accurately analyzes a character from world literature through the character's actions, as required by the prompt. The thesis is clear and there is support. However, the support is poorly elaborated and reveals a superficial understanding of the play. Organization is logical, but the style of the essay is characterized by monotonous sentence structure and basic diction. The writer has general control over the conventions of usage and mechanics, but there are minor spelling errors and more distracting errors like a fragment, a comma splice, and a couple of errors in agreement.

Six Trait Analytic Scale

Ratings

Ideas and Content: 3	**Word Choice: 3**
Organization: 3	**Sentence Fluency: 3**
Voice: 3	**Conventions: 4**

Comments: The writer's general purpose—to show how the character of Creon is revealed through his actions—is clear. There is some support, but it is not sufficiently elaborated. There is an introduction and a conclusion, but neither is particularly engaging and effective. Sequencing is logical. The writer's voice is sincere but the tone, generally objective, sometimes becomes personal, as when the writer refers to Creon as "stupid." The writer's choice of words is adequate, but not remarkable. Sentences are usually grammatically correct and easily understandable, but while there is some variety in sentence length and less in sentence structure, most sentences begin the same way. With the exception of a few misspelled words, a sentence fragment, a couple of errors in agreement, and a comma splice, the writer demonstrates an adaquate grasp of writing conventions.

Sample C: Literary Analysis

PROMPT

One way that writers reveal character is through the characters' actions. From the novels, short stories, plays, poems, and biographies you have read, select a work in which character is revealed by action. Describe the character and use specific references from the work to show how the character's actions reveal his or her nature. The work you choose must be from world literature other than British (England, Ireland, Scotland, Wales) literature and American (United States) literature.

Antigone is about a king named Creon. He got to be king after a war which killed the other King. He was named Eteocles. Creon made a law against buring the bodies of the people which fought against his city. Their religion said every body should be buried though. So Creon probably comitting a sin by making this law. Creon turned about to be a real bad king.

Anyway this girl named Antigone buried one of the bodies and broke the law. Because the body she buried was her brother and she said he was supposed to be buried. The gods wanted him to be. Creon was her uncle and he got real mad at her for buring the body so mad he said she had to be punished to death. There was another girl named Ismene who was the sister. She was afraid so her sister was mad at her.

Creon has a son named Haimon who wanted to marry Antigone, but he can't if his father kills her so he goes to his father to get him to let her go. He gets real mad at his father and threatens to kill him. When a blind man tells Creon that something bad is going to happen to him for what he did, Creon gets mad but later these men tell him the blind man has never been wrong. Creon gets scared. He went and buried the body. Then to let Antigone go. To late. Antigone hung herself. Haimon is there. When he sees his father he tries to stab him but misses and stabs himself on purpose insted. Then Creon is sorry and carrys Haimon back. When he gets there he finds out that his wife has stabbed herself, too. All this happens because Creon is a bad king.

Sample C Evaluation: Literary Analysis

Six Point Holistic Scale

Rating: 2 points

Comments: The essay addresses the prompt in that it deals with a character from world literature. However, the essay has a barely recognizable, perhaps accidental, thesis ("Creon turned about to be a real bad king") and ignores an important element of the prompt—how Creon's character is revealed by his actions. Support consists of a sketchy paraphrase of some of the major events of the work organized in a roughly chronological pattern. The writer's diction is limited and the sentence structure is simple and monotonous. Numerous serious errors in the conventions of usage and mechanics further weaken an already unacceptable essay.

Four Point Holistic Scale

Rating: 1 point

Comments: The essay fails to adequately address all the elements of the prompt. It contains a rough thesis—"Creon turned out to be a real bad king"—but it lacks both focus and organization, consisting mostly of a rough paraphrase in chronological order of some of the important events in the play. There is little control over sentence structure or diction, and even less over the conventions of mechanics and usage. Serious errors interfere with the reader's understanding.

Six Trait Analytic Scale

Ratings

Ideas and Content: 1	**Word Choice: 1**
Organization: 1	**Sentence Fluency: 1**
Voice: 3	**Conventions: 1**

Comments: While the paper begins and ends with Creon, there is no sense of purpose except, perhaps, to retell important events in the work. The sequencing is roughly chronological, but to no apparent end. The voice is sincere and somewhat engaging, giving the reader the sense that the paper is the writer's personal reaction to the characters and events depicted in the work. The writer's vocabulary is limited. Sentence structure lacks variety. Numerous errors in spelling, punctuation, usage and grammar make the paper somewhat difficult to read.

Notes on Literary Analyses

Use this page to jot down notes about the literary analyses or evaluations you
have just read. How would you evaluate the essays?

_____

_____

_____

_____

_____

_____

_____

_____

_____

_____

_____

_____

_____

_____

_____

_____

_____

_____

_____

_____

_____

_____

_____

_____

_____

_____

_____

_____

_____

_____

Making a Video Reflection

DIRECTIONS: Circle 1, 2, or 3 below to indicate your evaluation of each item.

Evaluation Scale:	1 = Not at all	2 = To some extent	3 = Successfully

- The student chooses an appropriate personal experience on which to base a video reflection.   1   2   3

- The student sketches, in storyboard format, the major events of the experience he or she has selected.   1   2   3

- The student's storyboard shows a clear and creative sequence of shots.   1   2   3

- The student effectively uses in-camera editing while taping his or her reflection.   1   2   3

- The student uses a variety of visual techniques to add interest and meaning.   1   2   3

- The student uses a variety of audio techniques to add interest and meaning.   1   2   3

- The video's use of lighting contributes to mood or adds clarity.   1   2   3

- The student responds productively to feedback from peers who have viewed his or her reflection.   1   2   3

- The student views his or her peers' reflections and provides constructive feedback.   1   2   3

Comparing and Contrasting Media Coverage

DIRECTIONS: Circle 1, 2, or 3 below to indicate your evaluation of each item.

▶ **Evaluation Scale:**   1 = Not at all   2 = To some extent   3 = Successfully

- The student locates two or more sources of news media coverage of the same event.   1   2   3

- The student lists the attention-getting techniques in each source.   1   2   3

- The student identifies point of view in each news item.   1   2   3

- The student evaluates how the attention-getting techniques in each source shape his or her impression of the event.   1   2   3

- The student assesses what his or her view of the event would be if he or she had seen only one of the sources.   1   2   3

- The student evaluates which source covered the event more thoroughly and accurately.   1   2   3

- The student uses evidence to support all answers.   1   2   3

- If asked, the student clearly presents his or her findings to the class, answers questions, and responds appropriately to feedback.   1   2   3

Analyzing the Effects of TV

DIRECTIONS: Circle 1, 2, or 3 below to indicate your evaluation of each item.

Evaluation Scale:	1 = Not at all	2 = To some extent	3 = Successfully

Names of group members:

_____

_____

_____

- The students brainstorm a list of three prominent careers depicted on television programs.   1   2   3

- The students identify the characteristics of each career according to how that career is represented on television.   1   2   3

- The students contact and record interviews with actual career practitioners, asking in particular about the characteristics the students have identified in television representations of the career.   1   2   3

- From their interview results, the students identify characteristics and other information omitted from the television representations of the careers they have researched.   1   2   3

- The students clearly present their results in a class report.   1   2   3

- Each student contributes to the group project.   1   2   3

RUBRIC

Giving an Informative Speech

DIRECTIONS: Circle 1, 2, or 3 below to indicate your evaluation of each item.

Evaluation Scale:	1 = Not at all	2 = To some extent	3 = Successfully

- The student considers the needs, background, and interests of his or her audience.   1   2   3

- The student logically organizes the details of his or her speech.   1   2   3

- The student uses an effective balance of standard and technical language.   1   2   3

- The student demonstrates enthusiasm.   1   2   3

- The student maintains eye contact with his or her audience.   1   2   3

- The student speaks clearly and audibly, using volume, vocal pitch, and rate of speaking to emphasize points and create interest.   1   2   3

- The speech includes effective visual aides or demonstrations.   1   2   3

- The speech is smooth and well rehearsed.   1   2   3

- The student effectively uses the question-and-answer time to ensure his or her message is understood.   1   2   3

- The student uses audience feedback to evaluate the presentation's effectiveness and to set goals for future presentations.   1   2   3

- When listening to classmates' speeches, the student takes notes, makes predictions and personal connections, and participates in the question-and-answer period.   1   2   3

Recognizing News Genres

DIRECTIONS: Circle 1, 2, or 3 below to indicate your evaluation of each item.

Evaluation Scale:	1 = Not at all	2 = To some extent	3 = Successfully

- The student critically views a national news broadcast, a news-magazine, and a documentary.   1   2   3

- The student's analysis specifies how much of each program is devoted to breaking news and how much is devoted to other types of stories.   1   2   3

- The student's analysis identifies what points of view or aspects of the topic are *not* represented in the programs.   1   2   3

- The student's analysis considers whether each news program provides factual evidence or relies on emotional reactions; the student provides evidence for his or her answers.   1   2   3

- The student's analysis identifies the purpose(s) of each news story and explains why he or she thinks so.   1   2   3

- The student records commercials aired during the broadcasts and thoughtfully identifies the target audience of selected commercials.   1   2   3

- The student's analysis indicates which of his or her own questions are left unanswered by the programs.   1   2   3

- The student's analysis notes which type of news program shows the least bias.   1   2   3

- The student decides whether each program provides sufficient coverage of the subjects on which it reports.   1   2   3

- Whether written or presented orally, the analysis is clear and logically organized.   1   2   3

Critiquing a Film

DIRECTIONS: Circle 1, 2, or 3 below to indicate your evaluation of each item.

Evaluation Scale:	1 = Not at all	2 = To some extent	3 = Successfully

- The student chooses an appropriate film to review. 1 2 3

- The student takes thorough notes on the filmmaker's use of literary elements such as point of view, setting, character, plot, and theme. 1 2 3

- The student takes thorough notes on the filmmaker's use of technical elements such as lighting, sound, and camera techniques. 1 2 3

- The student uses specific evaluation criteria to judge the effectiveness of the film's literary and technical elements. 1 2 3

- The student writes a critique based on his or her evaluation of the elements of the film. 1 2 3

- The critique cites specific evidence from the film. 1 2 3

- The critique is clearly and logically organized. 1 2 3

- The student contributes thoughtfully to group discussion of similarities and differences in group members' opinions of the films they have critiqued. 1 2 3

Presenting an Oral Interpretation

DIRECTIONS: Circle 1, 2, or 3 below to indicate your evaluation of each item.

Evaluation Scale:	1 = Not at all	2 = To some extent	3 = Successfully

- The student chooses an appropriate short story to interpret. 1 2 3

- The student introduces the interpretation with author, title, and any necessary background information. 1 2 3

- The student's interpretation shows a familiarity with the text. 1 2 3

- The student's interpretation reveals an understanding of the story's point of view. 1 2 3

- The student uses varied and appropriate gestures and facial expressions to tell the story. 1 2 3

- The student uses an effective pitch and tone of voice to convey meaning. 1 2 3

- The student maintains eye contact with listeners. 1 2 3

- The student uses audience feedback to evaluate the presentation's effectiveness and to set goals for future presentations. 1 2 3

- The student listens attentively to his or her peers' oral interpretations and provides appropriate feedback. 1 2 3

Evaluating Web Sites

DIRECTIONS: Circle 1, 2, or 3 below to indicate your evaluation of each item.

> **Evaluation Scale:**   1 = Not at all   2 = To some extent   3 = Successfully

Names of students working together:

_____

_____

- The students use a search engine to research specific topics.   1   2   3

- The students select three or four web sites to evaluate, considering   1   2   3
  which sites the search engine indicates are likely matches and noting
  the reliability of the sites' URLs.

- The students evaluate the sites' objectivity.   1   2   3

- The students evaluate the sites' reliability.   1   2   3

- The students evaluate the sites' completeness.   1   2   3

- The students evaluate the sites' clarity.   1   2   3

- The students evaluate whether the sites are reasonably current.   1   2   3

- The students evaluate the sites' accuracy.   1   2   3

- Based on the criteria-based judgments they have made, the students   1   2   3
  determine which site is most reliable and valid.

- The students clearly explain their judgments to the class and supply   1   2   3
  evidence for each evaluation.

- Each student contributes to the group project.   1   2   3

Analyzing Editorial Cartoons

DIRECTIONS: Circle 1, 2, or 3 below to indicate your evaluation of each item.

Evaluation Scale:	1 = Not at all	2 = To some extent	3 = Successfully

- The student selects an appropriate cartoon to analyze.   1   2   3

- The student identifies the issue the cartoon addresses and the   1   2   3
  cartoonist's opinion of the issue; the student provides evidence
  for his or her answers.

- The student correctly identifies symbolism, analogy, exaggeration or   1   2   3
  caricature, and irony in the cartoon and explains how each technique
  he or she finds contributes to the meaning of the cartoon.

- The student forms an opinion about whether the cartoon is or is not   1   2   3
  funny (and to whom) and supports his or her judgment.

- The student recognizes an alternative view to the issue addressed in   1   2   3
  the cartoon and suggests ways to revise the cartoon to show the
  alternative view.

Giving a Persuasive Speech

DIRECTIONS: Circle 1, 2, or 3 below to indicate your evaluation of each item.

Evaluation Scale:	1 = Not at all	2 = To some extent	3 = Successfully

Speaking:

- The student chooses an issue and considers task, occasion, and audience.   1   2   3

- The student clearly states a position.   1   2   3

- The student supports the position with sufficient and reliable evidence.   1   2   3

- The speech includes both logical and emotional appeals.   1   2   3

- The student uses an appropriate tone and effective rhetorical strategies.   1   2   3

- The student maintains eye contact with listeners.   1   2   3

- The student uses varied and appropriate gestures and facial expressions to emphasize ideas.   1   2   3

- The student uses good posture.   1   2   3

- The student demonstrates enthusiasm.   1   2   3

- The student enunciates words clearly and avoids vocalized pauses.   1   2   3

- The student speaks at a reasonable pitch, volume, and rate.   1   2   3

- The student uses audience feedback to evaluate the presentation's effectiveness and to set goals for future presentations.   1   2   3

Listening:

- The student uses clear and appropriate criteria to evaluate his or her peers' informative speeches.   1   2   3

- The student focuses on the speaker and notes any questions he or she has about the speech.   1   2   3

- The student provides constructive feedback to the speaker.   1   2   3

Making a Video Documentary

DIRECTIONS: Circle 1, 2, or 3 below to indicate your evaluation of each item.

Evaluation Scale:	1 = Not at all	2 = To some extent	3 = Successfully

- The student's documentary shows consideration of the needs, background, and interests of the audience.   1   2   3

- The documentary is five to seven minutes in length.   1   2   3

- The documentary clearly conveys a controlling idea or message.   1   2   3

- The documentary engages the audience's emotions.   1   2   3

- The documentary shows a clear sequence of shots.   1   2   3

- The documentary's scenes are a desirable length.   1   2   3

- The documentary's beginning captures the audience's attention; the ending leaves the desired impression.   1   2   3

- The student uses effective words, visual elements, and music.   1   2   3

- Interviews, if included, reinforce the documentary's controlling idea or message.   1   2   3

- The student uses basic video techniques to add variety and interest.   1   2   3

- The student creates and distributes questionnaires or feedback forms.   1   2   3

- The student uses audience feedback to evaluate the documentary's effectiveness and to set goals for future projects.   1   2   3

for **CHOICES** *page 15*   **RUBRICS**

Introduction: *Choices* Activities

Evaluation Scale:	1 = Not at all	2 = To some extent	3 = Successfully

Writing

1. A New View

	1	2	3
The student chooses a thoughtful and appropriate analogy for his or her writing process.	1	2	3
The student clearly states the comparison in a sentence and then sufficiently elaborates and explains the sentence.	1	2	3
The final essay shows a thorough understanding of the writing process.	1	2	3
The essay is clear and logically organized.	1	2	3
The essay is relatively free of errors in spelling, grammar, usage, and mechanics.	1	2	3
The student speaks audibly and clearly when presenting the essay to the class.	1	2	3

Collaborative Reading

2. Double the Process

	1	2	3
The students select an appropriate book and take turns reading it aloud.	1	2	3
Both students take an active role in reading and responding to the text and to each other.	1	2	3
The pair's oral report shows a thorough understanding of the reading process.	1	2	3
The report explains similarities and differences in the two students' processes and acknowledges which strategies they found especially effective.	1	2	3
The students speak audibly and clearly when sharing with the class.	1	2	3

Careers

3. Reading and Writing on the Job

	1	2	3
The group brainstorms occupations that involve reading and writing.	1	2	3
The group chooses an occupation to research and divides research tasks equitably.	1	2	3
The group's research identifies unique characteristics and tasks of the career.	1	2	3
The group's flier thoroughly explains how reading and writing contribute to success in the career.	1	2	3
The flier demonstrates the group's creativity and attention to detail.	1	2	3

Introduction: *Choices* Activities *(continued)*

Evaluation Scale:	1 = Not at all	2 = To some extent	3 = Successfully

Literature

4. Approaching Different Texts

- The student selects appropriate and varied passages to read.   1   2   3
- The student takes thoughtful notes on how his or her own reading   1   2   3
  process varies when reading different types of material.
- The student actively contributes to the group discussion.   1   2   3

Chapter One: *Choices* Activities

Evaluation Scale:	1 = Not at all	2 = To some extent	3 = Successfully

Crossing the Curriculum: Social Studies

1. Snatched from the Headlines

- The student selects an appropriate event featured in the media. 1 2 3
- The student creates a two-minute audio commentary that explains how the event described in the news story affects his or her life. 1 2 3
- The audio commentary includes specific details and thoughtful connections. 1 2 3
- The student speaks clearly, audibly, and expressively on the audio tape. 1 2 3

Literature

2. Join the Book Club

- The student selects an appropriate book. 1 2 3
- The student writes a one-hundred-word review that thoughtfully explains how the book has influenced him or her. 1 2 3
- The review uses appropriate passages for support. 1 2 3
- The review is clear and relatively free of errors in spelling, grammar, usage, and mechanics. 1 2 3
- The student posts his or her review on an online book club or online book store. 1 2 3

Careers

3. You're Hired!

- The student chooses a personal failure that prompted useful reflection of positive action. 1 2 3
- The student prepares a two-minute oral interview response that explains the failure and accompanying lesson. 1 2 3
- The response cites specifics and shows an appropriate awareness of purpose and audience. 1 2 3
- The student speaks audibly and clearly during the presentation. 1 2 3

Viewing and Representing

4. The Land That Time Forgot

- The student creates a series of illustrations that effectively document the important aspects of the student's life. 1 2 3
- The illustrations show an awareness of the audience—a viewer from the distant future. 1 2 3
- The illustrations are detailed and thoughtful representations of the student's unique perspective. 1 2 3
- The illustrations demonstrate the student's creativity. 1 2 3

Chapter Two: *Choices* Activities

Evaluation Scale:	1 = Not at all	2 = To some extent	3 = Successfully

Careers

1. Chart Your Future

- The student chooses two subjects that are related to the student's life after graduation.   1   2   3
- In an organized chart, the student lists all of the relevant features of the two subjects.   1   2   3
- For each relevant feature, the chart cites specific details and examples for each of the two subjects.   1   2   3
- The student writes a paragraph that carefully synthesizes the information from his or her chart.   1   2   3
- The chart and paragraph demonstrate the student's understanding of comparisons and contrasts.   1   2   3

Literature

2. Movie *vs.* Book

- The student selects a scene from a movie adaptation of a book and reads the corresponding portion of the book.   1   2   3
- The student thoughtfully chooses relevant features to compare, including literary elements such as characterization and plot.   1   2   3
- The student creates a graphic that shows similarities and differences between the movie and book.   1   2   3
- The student cites specific details and examples from the movie and book.   1   2   3
- The graphic is neat and well organized.   1   2   3

Speaking and Listening

3. People Are Talking

- The student selects a local or school event that he or she did not witness and interviews two witnesses separately.   1   2   3
- In a chart, the student thoughtfully compares and contrasts the two accounts.   1   2   3
- The student integrates the two accounts into his or her own retelling of the event.   1   2   3
- The audio account is comprehensive and clearly organized.   1   2   3
- The student speaks clearly and audibly on the audiotape.   1   2   3

Chapter Two: *Choices* Activities

Evaluation Scale:	1 = Not at all	2 = To some extent	3 = Successfully

Crossing the Curriculum: Science

4. Concentrate on Comparisons

- The student selects two similar-looking compounds.   1 2 3
- The student writes a clear and detailed explanation of how to tell the compounds apart.   1 2 3
- The explanation demonstrates the student's thorough understanding of how the compounds are distinct.   1 2 3
- The explanation demonstrates the student's understanding of comparison-contrast structure.   1 2 3
- The explanation is logically organized and relatively free of errors in spelling, usage, grammar, and mechanics.   1 2 3

Chapter Three: *Choices* Activities

Evaluation Scale:	1 = Not at all	2 = To some extent	3 = Successfully

Careers

1. To Be or Not to Be

- The student selects a career to analyze and does sufficient research to understand its pros and cons.   1   2   3
- The student identifies three positive and negative effects this career choice might have on his or her life.   1   2   3
- The student creates a poster that clearly explains or illustrates the pros and cons of the career choice.   1   2   3
- The poster is neat and creatively composed.   1   2   3

Viewing and Representing

2. A Double Take

- The student chooses and videotapes a nightly news report involving causes and effects.   1   2   3
- The student takes careful and accurate notes on the causes and effects in the report.   1   2   3
- The student identifies examples of oversimplification and false cause-and-effect relationships in the news report.   1   2   3
- The student prepares a short oral presentation about the news story that demonstrates the student's understanding of cause-and-effect relationships.   1   2   3
- The student speaks clearly and audibly during the presentation.   1   2   3

Crossing the Curriculum: Arts & Science

3. Make It Work!

- The students brainstorm a complicated process to perform a simple task.   1   2   3
- The students plan and execute a drawing that shows how a Rube Goldberg-like machine will accomplish the task in at least five steps.   1   2   3
- The drawing demonstrates the students' creativity.   1   2   3
- The students clearly explain the causal chain to the class.   1   2   3
- Each student actively contributes to the group project.   1   2   3

Chapter Three: *Choices* Activities *(continued)*

> **Evaluation Scale:**   1 = Not at all   2 = To some extent   3 = Successfully

Crossing the Curriculum: Literature

4. Motivations and Consequences

- The student selects an appropriate work of fiction and writes an analysis of the motives of the characters.   1   2   3

- The analysis in a detailed way notes the effects each character has on fellow characters or the plot of the story.   1   2   3

- The analysis demonstrates the student's understanding of cause-and-effect relationships.   1   2   3

- The analysis is logically organized and relatively free of errors in spelling, usage, grammar, and mechanics.   1   2   3

Chapter Four: *Choices* Activities

▶ **Evaluation Scale:**   1 = Not at all   2 = To some extent   3 = Successfully

Careers

1. Give a Check-Up

- The student prepares thoughtful questions and conducts an interview   1   2   3
  with a health professional about the health problems the professional
  treats.
- In a brief oral report, the student explains his or her interview results,   1   2   3
  noting in particular any typical health problems, treatments, and
  research methods.
- The report is comprehensive and clearly and logically organized.   1   2   3
- The student speaks clearly and audibly during the presentation.   1   2   3

Crossing the Curriculum: Literature

2. Hatch a Plot

- The student writes a brief summary of a short-story plot based on a   1   2   3
  problem he or she finds interesting.
- The responses of the story's main character create a conflict which is   1   2   3
  resolved by the story's end.
- The summary shows creativity and an awareness of literary elements.   1   2   3
- The summary is clearly organized and relatively free of errors in   1   2   3
  spelling, grammar, usage, and mechanics.

Speaking and Listening

3. Join the Debate

- The student attends a debate practice or competition and takes notes   1   2   3
  on how the debaters discuss the problems they have researched.
- The student notes (and, if necessary, conducts research on) the rules of   1   2   3
  debate and identifies how participants maintain composure in debate
  situations.
- The student notes how debaters present effective solutions to problems.   1   2   3
- The student uses his or her findings to create a detailed debate "how-to"   1   2   3
  booklet.
- The booklet is clearly organized and relatively free of errors in spelling, 1   2   3
  grammar, usage, and mechanics.

Chapter Four: *Choices* Activities *(continued)*

> **Evaluation Scale:**   1 = Not at all   2 = To some extent   3 = Successfully

Media and Technology

4. Tune It In

- The student watches or listens to a broadcast of a governmental proceeding.   1   2   3

- The student carefully notes the problems discussed and the people discussing the problems.   1   2   3

- The student notes any solutions discussed, and identifies the ways government officials try to solve problems.   1   2   3

- The student's final profile demonstrates the student's understanding of problem-solution analysis.   1   2   3

- The profile is relatively free of errors in spelling, grammar, usage, and mechanics.   1   2   3

Chapter Five: *Choices* Activities

▶ **Evaluation Scale:**   1 = Not at all   2 = To some extent   3 = Successfully

Careers

1. Analysis at Work

■ The student identifies a prospective career and writes a paragraph detailing how he or she could use analysis skills in this career.	1	2	3
■ The paragraph demonstrates an accurate understanding of the career.	1	2	3
■ The paragraph demonstrates an understanding of analysis.	1	2	3
■ The paragraph is clearly organized and relatively free of errors in usage, grammar, spelling, and mechanics.	1	2	3

Speaking and Listening

2. Discover Writing Strategies

■ The student attends a professional reading and asks the writer thoughtful and specific questions about his or her writing strategies. (Alternatively, the student mails his or her questions to the writer.)	1	2	3
■ The student creates a checklist that includes both his or her own writing strategies and the strategies learned from the professional writer.	1	2	3
■ The checklist demonstrates the student's understanding of writing strategies and why they are used.	1	2	3
■ The student distributes the checklist to others and solicits feedback.	1	2	3

Media and Technology

3. Analyze an Analysis

■ The student selects an appropriate review to analyze.	1	2	3
■ The student creates a graphic organizer that thoughtfully lists strengths and weaknesses of subject being reviewed as well as other points of interest.	1	2	3
■ The student discusses his or her organizer with other students.	1	2	3

Viewing and Representing

4. Illustrate a Children's Book

■ The student creates an illustrated children's book that demonstrates an attention to plot, character, setting, and point of view.	1	2	3
■ The student chooses interesting characters and key events to illustrate.	1	2	3
■ The student's story is appropriate for children.	1	2	3
■ The book demonstrates the student's creativity.	1	2	3
■ The children's book is free of errors in usage, grammar, spelling, and mechanics.	1	2	3
■ The student shares his or her book with students in a local elementary school.	1	2	3

for **CHOICES**   *page 249*   **RUBRICS**

Chapter Six: *Choices* Activities

▶ **Evaluation Scale:**   1 = Not at all   2 = To some extent   3 = Successfully

Careers

1. Research Your Future

- The student selects a career to research and creates appropriate questions   1 2 3
  about the field, including how research strategies are used in the field.
- The student chooses reliable sources in which to research the career and   1 2 3
  takes careful notes.
- The student's oral or video presentation is clear and thorough.   1 2 3

Literature

2. Your Very Own Book Club

- The student selects an author and researches the author's life and   1 2 3
  influences.
- The student notes similarities between events, themes, or character   1 2 3
  types in the author's writing and personal life.
- The student writes a personal letter that clearly explains the student's   1 2 3
  conclusions and shows an awareness of audience.
- The student's letter is correctly formatted and relatively free of errors   1 2 3
  in spelling, grammar, usage, and mechanics.

Crossing the Curriculum: The Arts

3. Your Art Form

- The student writes a sentence that explains the personal appeal of his   1 2 3
  or her selected art form.
- The student locates reliable Web sites to use in researching the art form   1 2 3
  and in locating diverse views on the art form.
- The student's paragraph carefully synthesizes the student's views and   1 2 3
  those of others.
- The paragraph is logically organized and relatively free of errors in   1 2 3
  spelling, grammar, usage, and mechanics.

Media and Technology

4. One Research Report Leads to Another

- With classmates, the student compiles a set of research questions   1 2 3
  suggested by each group member's report.
- Each student selects a question from the list and conducts online research.   1 2 3
- The student writes a clear and organized early plan for a possible group   1 2 3
  research report.
- The plan demonstrates the student's careful thinking about the subject   1 2 3
  and understanding of the tasks necessary in preparing a research report.

Chapter Seven: *Choices* Activities

Evaluation Scale: 1 = Not at all   2 = To some extent   3 = Successfully

Careers

1. Persuasion That Pays

- The student prepares a thoughtful list of interview questions.   1   2   3
- The student contacts and interviews an appropriate professional.   1   2   3
- The student writes a paragraph discussing specific writing strategies and persuasive skills involved in the professional's daily work.   1   2   3
- The paragraph includes the pertinent elements of the interview.   1   2   3
- The paragraph is clearly and logically organized.   1   2   3
- The paragraph is relatively free of errors in spelling, usage, grammar, and mechanics.   1   2   3

Literature

2. Poetically Persuasive

- The student drafts a persuasive poem or song lyric that includes a clear position and adequate support.   1   2   3
- The poem or song lyric demonstrates the student's understanding of poetic elements.   1   2   3
- The poem or song lyric demonstrates the student's creativity.   1   2   3
- The message of the poem or song lyric is clearly presented.   1   2   3

Media and Technology

3. Web of Persuasion

- The student researches Web sites that express an opinion and considers their persuasive strategies.   1   2   3
- The student creates a persuasive Web page based on his or her persuasive essay.   1   2   3
- The Web page clearly states an opinion and issues a call to action.   1   2   3
- The Web page shows attention to how title, photos, and text can contribute to the student's persuasive purpose.   1   2   3
- The Web page is logically organized and relatively free of errors in spelling, usage, grammar, and mechanics.   1   2   3

Chapter Seven: *Choices* Activities *(continued)*

▶ **Evaluation Scale:**   1 = Not at all   2 = To some extent   3 = Successfully

Crossing the Curriculum: Journalism

4. Editorially Yours

- The student selects an appropriate topic for an editorial.   1   2   3
- The student writes an editorial clearly expressing his or her opinion.   1   2   3
- The editorial uses persuasive appeals and, if appropriate, issues a
  call to action.   1   2   3
- The editorial demonstrates the student's research and knowledge of the
  subject matter.   1   2   3
- The editorial reflects the student's awareness of the typical form and
  tone of editorials.   1   2   3
- The editorial is logically organized and relatively free of errors in
  spelling, usage, grammar, and mechanics.   1   2   3

Art

5. In Your Opinion

- The student creates a cartoon that clearly shows his or her opinion on
  his or her topic.   1   2   3
- The student effectively uses common editorial cartoon elements such as
  symbolism, analogy, exaggeration or caricature, and irony.   1   2   3
- The cartoon demonstrates the student's creativity.   1   2   3

Chapter Eight: *Choices* Activities

▶ | **Evaluation Scale:** | 1 = Not at all | 2 = To some extent | 3 = Successfully |

Careers

1. In the Ad Game

- The student prepares a comprehensive list of interview questions about the writing process.   1   2   3
- The student contacts and interviews an appropriate professional.   1   2   3
- The student's presentation clearly explains the professional's prewriting, writing, and revision strategies.   1   2   3
- The presentation describes the rewards and challenges of this kind of work and cites pertinent details and quotations from the interview.   1   2   3
- The presentation is clearly and logically organized.   1   2   3
- The student speaks clearly and audibly during his or her presentation.   1   2   3

Literature

2. Come to Sunny Mars

- The student chooses a particular book's setting for his or her print advertisement.   1   2   3
- The student's ad contains lively and persuasive text and appeals designed to interest the target audience.   1   2   3
- The ad uses appealing illustrations, color, and other design features.   1   2   3
- The ad demonstrates the student's understanding of the persuasive elements of advertising.   1   2   3
- The ad demonstrates the student's creativity.   1   2   3
- The ad is neat and free of errors in spelling, usage, grammar, and mechanics.   1   2   3

Crossing the Curriculum: History

3. Rabble-Rousing

- The student selects an appropriate historical movement.   1   2   3
- The student's brochure uses logical and emotional appeals and other appropriate persuasive strategies to convince others to join the movement.   1   2   3
- The brochure demonstrates the student's understanding of the historical event.   1   2   3
- The brochure shows the student's creativity.   1   2   3
- The brochure is neat and relatively free of errors in spelling, usage, grammar, and mechanics.   1   2   3

Chapter Eight: *Choices* Activities *(continued)*

▶ **Evaluation Scale:**   1 = Not at all   2 = To some extent   3 = Successfully

Media and Technology

4. Apples vs. Oranges

- The student selects a product that is widely advertised.   1   2   3
- The student finds examples of the advertising campaign in different   1   2   3
  media.
- In a chart, the student thoughtfully compares and contrasts the   1   2   3
  persuasive elements of the various ads.
- The student's oral presentation effectively explains which form of   1   2   3
  advertising he or she feels is most effective and why.
- The student supports his or her conclusion with evidence from the   1   2   3
  advertisements.
- The student speaks clearly and audibly during the presentation.   1   2   3